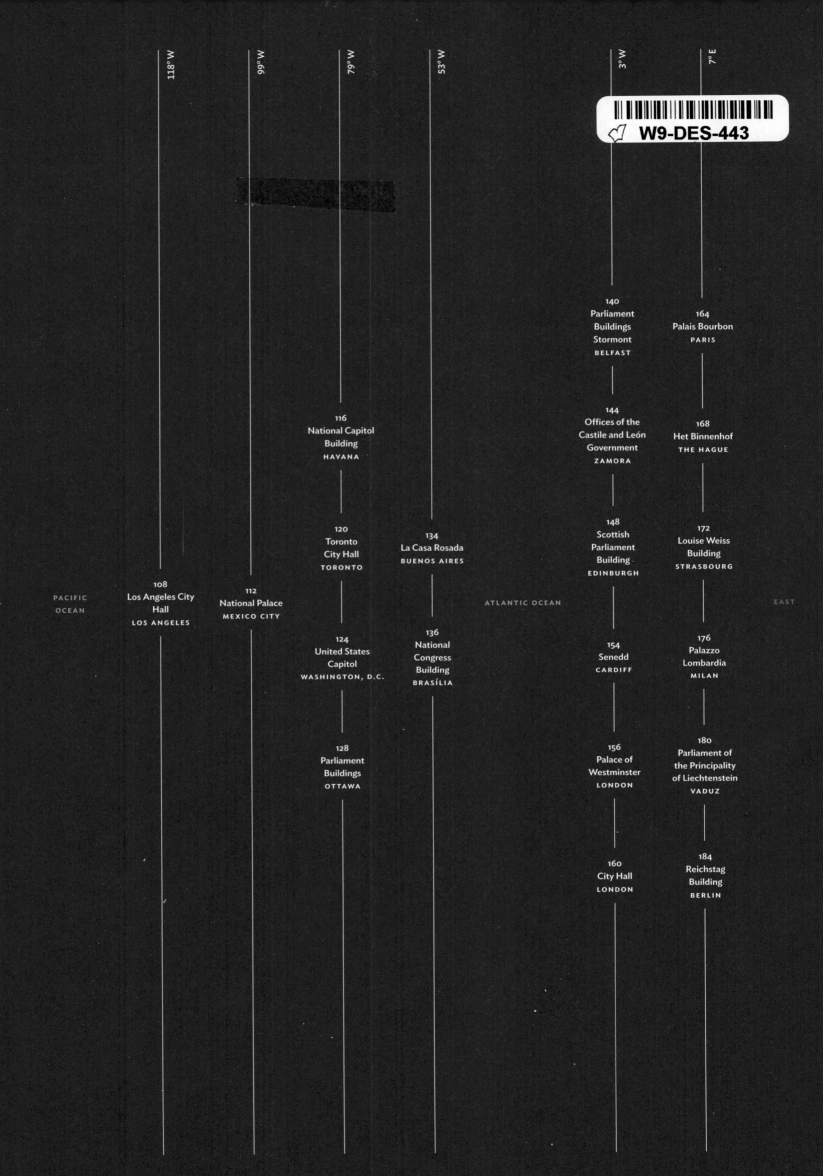

118° W

99° W

79° W

53° W

3° W

7° E

140
Parliament
Buildings
Stormont
BELFAST

164
Palais Bourbon
PARIS

144
Offices of the
Castile and León
Government
ZAMORA

168
Het Binnenhof
THE HAGUE

116
National Capitol
Building
HAVANA

120
Toronto
City Hall
TORONTO

134
La Casa Rosada
BUENOS AIRES

148
Scottish
Parliament
Building
EDINBURGH

172
Louise Weiss
Building
STRASBOURG

PACIFIC
OCEAN

108
Los Angeles City
Hall
LOS ANGELES

112
National Palace
MEXICO CITY

ATLANTIC OCEAN

EAST

124
United States
Capitol
WASHINGTON, D.C.

136
National
Congress
Building
BRASÍLIA

154
Senedd
CARDIFF

176
Palazzo
Lombardia
MILAN

128
Parliament
Buildings
OTTAWA

156
Palace of
Westminster
LONDON

180
Parliament of
the Principality
of Liechtenstein
VADUZ

160
City Hall
LONDON

184
Reichstag
Building
BERLIN

ROADS Publishing
19–22 Dame Street
Dublin 2
Ireland

www.roads.co

First published 2015

1

Government
ROADS Reflections
Text copyright © ROADS Publishing
Design and layout copyright © ROADS Publishing
Image copyright © the copyright holders; see p. 189
Design by Conor & David

Printed in Turkey

Upper front-cover image:
Reichstag Dome, Berlin, Germany
© Kenneth C. Zirkel / Getty Images
Lower front-cover image:
Confederation Hall, Parliament Building, Ottawa, Canada
© De Agostini / R. Portolese / Getty Images
Back cover image:
The Great Hall of the People, Beijing, China
© Luis Castaneda Inc / The Image Bank / Getty Images

978-1-909399-45-7

GOVERNMENT

ROADS

PUBLISHING

Foreword

Ivan Harbour
Rogers Stirk Harbour + Partners

It is a unique challenge for an architect to be under the spotlight of public opinion and maelstrom of political debate that surrounds the design of a government building. Creating the Senedd (the National Assembly for Wales) in Cardiff was a once in a lifetime experience for myself and everyone involved at Rogers Stirk Harbour + Partners (RSHP). The Palace of Westminster in London was famously 300 per cent over budget and took five times as long to build than estimated. Neither of its architects, Charles Barry and Augustus Pugin, lived to see it completed; by all accounts it was a life-consuming work and a salutary lesson for those to follow. The Senedd is only a tiny building in comparison but I survived the process, although not without a fair share of drama, pleasure and pain.

For architects, a political body as a client is a peculiar beast. We have the pleasure of working closely and in confidence with all our clients; we forge long-term relationships as we help to guide them through their commissions. It is an enormous team effort and they are critical to that team. However in the UK, architecture is rarely a politician's pastime and there are few architects who have made the transition into full-time politics. The journey to deliver the Senedd saw numerous elected officials come and go but we eventually arrived at a handful of members from different parties, together with seasoned civil servants, whose common ground was a love of architecture. It was this team that made the Senedd happen and it is a team like this – with a passion for the built environment – that is critical to the success of any public project.

The architects of public buildings are usually selected through open consultation; in the Senedd's case this process involved a shortlisting, followed by an interview and an eventual limited but paid competition. In this case, they sought only the idea. A presentation by each competitor was then made to a panel of luminaries, chaired by former Prime Minister James Callaghan (Lord Callaghan of Cardiff) assisted by architectural advisers.

This enabled any questions to be answered there and then, and allowed the ideas to be clarified. The process constructed a level playing field to deliver the most appropriate concept.

Accompanying the design brief for the Senedd was a short foreword by Callaghan that stated the ambitions of Wales as a country and how they hoped this might be reflected in the new seat of government:

'This competition offers the architectural profession the opportunity to express a concept of what form should be assumed by a democratic assembly listening to and leading a small democratic nation as we enter the next millennium ... we would dare to hope that it will become a visible symbol, recognised and respected throughout the world, whenever the name of Wales is used.'

It was an illuminating and poignant statement and one that neatly captured what should be the aspiration for any new seat of government, regardless of scale.

Architects are used to working within tight constraints, indeed quite often the more constraints the more ingenious the solution and the more rooted in place a proposed building can become. The pressure of expectation from Callaghan's short piece, combined with a site of relatively few physical constraints – a business park in Cardiff's disused docks – produced an unusual situation that, on first sight, might have favoured symbols and emblems over context and place.

Architecture – particularly that of government buildings – always has a political context and, in the case of the Senedd, it was clear that, given the very public airing of the Welsh appetite for devolution (demonstrated through the ballot box in the successful Welsh devolution referendum in 1997), coupled with the subsequent argument over which city would host the new Assembly, the architecture would require a response that encouraged participation and make a gesture beyond the site.

These unique conditions for RSHP's most public building since the Centre Pompidou in Paris (1977) became the catalyst for a design that would deliver a distinctive seat of government for Wales.

We chose not to adopt aesthetic metaphors, symbols or historic motifs – often the architect's easy answer to appease historicists and anxiety over authenticity – but to define the building as a strict response to two fundamental questions: how could we place it on the site to suggest that the connection between building and land was without boundary? And how could we organise the public and private space to encourage participation between the elected body and the public electorate?

Our answer was to look beyond the initially mundane site and outwards to the sea, to the rest of the country and to the world beyond. We envisaged the site as an extension of the body of water, not a boundary to it. The building's concept was deceptively simple: a single, flowing public space, stretching from the water's edge over the space for the elected body, enabling a broad interface between the two and encouraging public engagement in a political space. The building would be anchored, internally, to its site and would also be outward looking. A canopy floating over the public space would give an indeterminate edge to the enclosure, belying the small scale of the building among its neighbours and extending its influence to the water's edge. A strong concept, we believed, for the expected ride ahead. And it would soon prove critical that it was.

I am reminded of the first meeting we had, soon after RSHP (then Richard Rogers Partnership) was announced as winners of the competition in October 1998. A team from the Welsh office arrived at our studio in Hammersmith, West London, and asked when we could start developing the design for construction. We politely suggested that we had only conceived of an idea and it would take many months of refinement, in collaboration with them, to make the idea a reality. They had not factored this collaborative exploration into their process and could not say, at that time, who would be able to make decisions to help us get there. The Secretary of State for Wales Ron Davies had just resigned and, in short, they thought we had completed our design during the competition.

The encounter underlined to us a key factor inherent in the design on any new home for political leadership: that it can often be a more emotional affair than any work undertaken with a business-orientated, private-sector client, and more so even than other civic building programmes, such as we experienced in our law courts for Bordeaux and Antwerp. A private client – accountable, in the main, only to itself – has a freedom to make decisions not afforded the political establishment.

Despite this heightened client connection, however, it proved difficult to extract critical comment that would start a debate on the concept. With no precedent other than a wish that the building promote co-operation rather than the confrontational arrangement of the Palace of Westminster (opposing parties sat facing each other), the entire client and consultant team had little or no experience to draw on to move the design forward. It was only when an external organisation, representing a number of disability groups, rightly raised their concerns about the concept while it was on public exhibition that a critical discourse was entered into that ultimately evolved the idea into its final form.

The re-presented design was finally endorsed by Rhodri Morgan, the third First Minister for Wales in as many years. Only a simple, clear and strong design concept – a critical characteristic, I feel, for any public building design to be successful – could have survived this tumultuous process, and it proved a significant affirmation of the potency of the original idea that it did so. The building's aesthetic was a direct consequence of this concept, allowing us to steer it through the approval process without the repeated subjective debates often levelled at overly symbolic designs. The Senedd was the future, not hewn by history but distinctly of the present, forging its own precedent.

I have talked about physical constraints positively driving design, but in the public arena politicians' pledges introduce new constraints that, while raising standards, can take a building into unknown territory. As architects we are aware of two construction constants: that building regulations exist to ensure that standards are universal and that legislation ensures a free market for products and services. Politicians' pledges, although grounded in good intention, can disrupt these constants. A commitment to exemplary sustainable performance and an inflexible desire to build a Welsh building from only Welsh material, even if unavailable, complicated the pre-set budgetary allowances. Outside influences can disrupt even the most carefully planned project if no room for manoeuvre is allowed for, and in our case we had unprecedented security conditions to factor in after the 9/11 terrorist attacks.

In the development of the Senedd, these issues were faced without the opportunity for debate over the balance of cost, time and quality. No aspect was flexible as the politicians had made their promises on them all. We know from a wealth of experience that without this flexibility a building project can be easily derailed. There is always common agreement on quality but the importance of both speed and cost are usually variable, determined not solely on material costs but on procurement processes and types of risk as well.

Looming over all civic projects is the gaze of public scrutiny, the much-repeated argument over costs; would it be better to 'spend the money on a new hospital rather than an expensive talking shop for politicians we never wanted'? A public building is an easy target and any uncertainty over the final cost can become the simplest shot of all.

Public buildings and the discussions about cost are always framed around bad news: over spend, over budget, overrun. Fortunately for the Senedd, the Scottish Parliament Building, Edinburgh, by EMBT and RMJM, was being delivered on a similar timescale and, by a real-time comparison of construction cost per square metre, we were able to demonstrate the Senedd was good value. The political debate continued, however, and ultimately the constant strain caused the project to stall.

By their nature, new parliament buildings are few in number. They are a unique career opportunity for an architect and a particular honour to be selected to design. In the construction industry, building costs are generally estimated by continuous benchmarking against similar projects – it allows the professional team to understand the quality desired and whether this is consistent with a client's ambitions – but their relative rarity meant there were no recently constructed parliament buildings in the UK when we set about our design for the Senedd. The two comparable projects, the Scottish Parliament Building and the Greater London Authority headquarters (City Hall), by Foster + Partners, were on the drawing board concurrently with the Senedd. Benchmarking our building as a whole was simply not possible and the alternative, benchmarking elements, was complicated by the Senedd's exemplar demands for design life, sustainability, access, security and material.

Soon after the project started on site it became clear that the Assembly's procurement process – based around the phased release of information, a process normally adopted when speed is of the essence, and without the security of benchmarking costs – risked a dramatic increase in the building's budget.

Due to a complex set of reasons we were very publicly removed from the job. We had suggested the procurement method was wrong and that it would inherently lead to cost overruns if pursued. Our eventual re-employment as the architect under a design and build contract substantiated our position.

The Assembly empowered an official who had recent project delivery experience and it was this guidance that brought focus to their decision-making, removing emotion and fixing the brief. This then gave us time to complete the full building design and allowed the builder to agree a fixed-price contract. This new process revealed that there was some flexibility after all: time. The newfound understanding allowed the project to proceed to completion without further incident.

The Senedd was the first building that RSHP were involved in that adopted a sustainable approach across the entire project, from embodied energy, material choices and construction practice, to energy-in-use and design life; factors that led, unusually, to a single-glazed naturally ventilated building.

The liberal use of Welsh slate was justifiable in embodied energy terms over other sources but other materials did not make the cut. There simply was not enough Welsh Forest-Stewardship-Council-approved oak available for the roof. We reserved its use for the furniture instead. We were able to steer dramatically away from the UK government's standard building brief of punched windows in solid walls and blast net curtains to a more open environment by providing a comprehensive proposal for security. This move also helped deliver the biggest change to the physical setting: a business park transformed into a waterside public space; a national asset for the people of Wales.

The result? Well it took twice as long to build and cost twice as much per square metre than imagined at the outset, but importantly, at the end, the National Audit Office confirmed to the Assembly that the Senedd was good value for money.

The Palace of Westminster, the Senedd; they both have histories, only the Senedd's is fresher in the mind. During the final stages of the troubled construction at Westminster, Pugin descended into madness following the submission of his design for the clock tower, known as Big Ben. While, unlike poor Pugin, I was never close to a hospital bed in Bedlam, I can empathise with the complexities of a government project that may have driven him there. The public buildings featuring in this book will all have similar stories to tell that demonstrate the determination of many to realise their existence. I have great admiration for all those involved, and their particular dedication and tolerance to working under such great public scrutiny.

Vorwort

Für einen Architekten kommt es einer einzigartigen Herausforderung gleich, sich im Brennpunkt der öffentlichen Meinung sowie im Mahlstrom der politischen Debatte zu finden, die mit dem Entwurf eines Regierungsgebäudes einhergeht. Die Erschaffung des Senedd (der Nationalversammlung von Wales) in Cardiff war für mich und alle am Projekt beteiligten Personen von Rogers Stirk Harbour + Partners (RSHP) eine einzigartige Erfahrung. Bekanntlich überstieg der Palace of Westminster in London sein Budget um 300 Prozent und dauerte seine Errichtung fünf Mal länger als veranschlagt. Von den Architekten Charles Barry und Augustus Pugin erlebte keiner seine Fertigstellung; in jeder Hinsicht war es ein langwieriges Unterfangen und eine heilsame Lektion für alles, was folgte. Im Vergleich dazu nimmt sich der Senedd recht bescheiden aus, mit dem Unterschied, dass ich die Fertigstellung erlebte, wenn auch mit einem gerüttelt Maß an Hysterie, Vergnügen und Qual.

Für Architekten ist ein Regierungsgebäude ein äußerst eigenwilliges Betätigungsfeld. Glücklicherweise arbeiten wir eng und in vollstem gegenseitigen Vertrauen mit unseren Auftraggebern zusammen; wir unterstützen sie bei der Umsetzung ihrer Vorhaben und knüpfen auf diese Weise dauerhafte Bande. Dies bedeutet eine enorme, aber für dieses Team ausschlaggebende Gruppenanstrengung. In Großbritannien beschäftigen sich jedoch äußerst wenige Politiker mit Architektur und nur eine Handvoll Architekten haben den Schritt hin zu Vollzeitpolitikern gewagt. Während des Entstehungsprozesses des Senedd kamen und gingen zahlreiche gewählte Volksvertreter, doch gelang es uns schließlich, einige Mitglieder einzelner Parteien sowie bewährte Staatsbedienstete zusammenzubringen, die eine gemeinsame Leidenschaft für Architektur verband. Diesem Team verdankt sich letztendlich der Senedd und der Erfolg jedes öffentlichen Vorhabens hängt unmittelbar von einer vergleichbaren Gruppe von Menschen mit einer Begeisterung für erbaute Umgebung ab.

Architekten öffentlicher Gebäude gehen für gewöhnlich aus öffentlichen Anhörungen hervor; im Fall des Senedd umfasste dieser Prozess eine Bewerberauswahl, gefolgt von einer Unterredung und einem eingeschränkten aber vergüteten Wettbewerb. Doch ging es dabei lediglich darum, den Entwurf auszuwählen. Anschließend hatte jeder Bewerber die Möglichkeit, einem Expertengremium unter dem Vorsitz des früheren Premierministers James Callaghan (Lord Callaghan of Cardiff), dem Architekturberater zur Seite standen, seinen Entwurf zu präsentieren. Dies ermöglichte die umgehende Beantwortung sämtlicher Fragen sowie die Klärung jeder einzelnen Idee. Der Prozess fußte auf einer Spielfläche auf Augenhöhe, die dem stimmigsten Konzept zum Durchbruch verhelfen sollte.

Begleitet wurde der Auslobungstext zum Senedd von einem kurzen Vorwort Callaghans, das die Ambitionen von Wales als Land unterstrich sowie die Hoffnung, der neue Regierungssitz möge diese Bestrebungen widerspiegeln:

„Dieser Wettbewerb bietet der Architur die Gelegenheit, einen Entwurf jener Gestalt vorzulegen, die einer demokratischen Nationalversammlung angemessen erscheint, welche einer kleinen demokratischen Nation dient und diese in das neue Jahrtausend führt... wir hegen die Hoffnung, dass sie sich zu einem sichtbaren Symbol entwickeln und bei der Nennung des Namens Wales in der Welt Anerkennung und Respekt hervorrufen wird. "

Diese aufschlussreiche und ergreifende Aussage fasste jenen Anspruch geschickt in Worte, der jedem neuen Regierungssitz, unabhängig von seiner Größe, zugrunde liegen sollte.

Architekten sind es gewohnt, ihre Arbeit an rigorose Zwänge anzupassen; umgekehrt gilt häufig sogar, dass eine Lösung umso genialer bzw. die Verwurzelung eines vorgeschlagenen Bauwerks mit seinem Standort umso tiefer ausfällt, je mehr Zwänge überwunden werden mussten. Der Erwartungsdruck, der aus Callaghans kurzer Rede

Avant-propos

Quel défi plus grand pour un architecte que celui de concevoir un bâtiment public officiel sous les feux de l'opinion publique et de l'arène politique ? Imaginer la Senedd (l'Assemblée nationale du pays de Galles) à Cardiff fut pour moi et pour tous les collaborateurs du cabinet Rogers Stirk Harbour + Partners (RSHP) ayant pris part au projet une expérience que l'on ne fait qu'une seule fois dans sa vie. La construction du palais de Westminster à Londres est restée dans les annales pour avoir dépassé son budget initial de 300 pour cent et duré cinq fois plus longtemps que prévu. Aucun de ses architectes, Charles Barry et Auguste Pugin, n'a vécu assez longtemps pour voir l'édifice achevé. À tous points de vue, cet ouvrage de toute une vie est un parfait exemple de sacerdoce à suivre. Si l'envergure de la Senedd n'a rien de comparable, j'ai toutefois mené sa construction jusqu'à son terme, non sans peine, avec son lot de douleur et de joie.

Les institutions politiques sont pour tout architecte des donneurs d'ordres particulièrement spéciaux. Nous avons la chance de travailler en toute confiance au contact étroit de tous nos clients ; nous nouons des relations durables dans la mesure où nous les guidons tout au long de leur commande. Ce type de missions exige un véritable travail d'équipe et sont essentielles pour l'esprit d'équipe. Pour autant, au Royaume-Uni, l'architecture n'est pas le passe-temps usuel des politiques, et peu d'architectes ont réussi à percer dans la politique. Le projet de construction de la Senedd a vu défiler un grand nombre d'élus, mais nous sommes finalement parvenus à ne retenir que quelques membres seulement des différentes parties impliquées, aidés de fonctionnaires chevronnés, tous ayant en commun une passion pour l'architecture. C'est grâce à cette équipe que la Senedd a vu le jour, et ce sont des équipes comme celle-ci, passionnée d'urbanisme, qui déterminent la réussite d'un projet public.

Les architectes de bâtiments publics sont générale-ment choisis à l'issue de consultations ouvertes. Dans le cas de la Senedd, les candidats préalablement sélectionnés ont ensuite passé un entretien, puis un concours final, limité mais rémunéré. Dans ce cas de figure, les donneurs d'ordres ne fondent leur choix que sur le concept général du projet. Chaque candidat a ensuite présenté son projet devant un jury de personnalités présidé par l'ancien Ministre James Callaghan (Lord Callaghan de Cardiff) assisté de conseillers en architecture. Ce processus a permis de répondre à toutes les questions soulevées et de clarifier les idées. Il a également contribué à instaurer des règles du jeu équitables dans la définition du concept le plus approprié au lieu.

La maquette d'avant projet fut précédée d'un bref avant propos par Lord Callaghan en personne dans lequel il a rappelé les ambitions du pays de Galles en tant que nation et l'espoir que le nouveau siège du gouvernement soit à la hauteur de telles aspirations :

« Ce concours offre aux architectes l'incroyable opportunité de donner corps à ce que devrait incarner une Assemblée démocratique à l'écoute de la modeste nation démocratique qu'elle entend diriger à l'aube de ce nouveau millénaire ... nous osons espérer que ce bâtiment deviendra un symbole visible, reconnu et respecté dans le monde entier, et portera haut et fort les valeurs du pays de Galles. »

Ce discours aussi éloquent qu'émouvant résume avec justesse ce à quoi est censé aspirer le nouveau siège d'un gouvernement, quelle que soit son importance.

Les architectes ont l'habitude de travailler sous de sévères contraintes, et force est de constater que plus le projet est soumis à des restrictions, plus la solution est bien souvent ingénieuse et le bâtiment proposé a plus de chances d'être étroitement ancré dans sa localité. L'énorme pression exprimée par Lord Callaghan dans son allocution, à laquelle s'ajoute le choix d'un site ne présentant que relativement peu de contraintes physiques – une zone d'affaires dans des

Prólogo

Para un arquitecto, estar en la mira de la opinión pública y en medio de la vorágine del debate político que gira alrededor del diseño de un edificio gubernamental constituye todo un reto. La creación del Senedd (la Asamblea Nacional de Gales) en Cardiff supuso una experiencia única en la vida tanto para mí como para todos los que participaron en Rogers Stirk Harbour + Partners (RSHP). El Palacio de Westminster de Londres se hizo famoso por superar en un 300 por ciento el presupuesto inicial y por tardar cinco veces más en construirse que el tiempo previsto. Ninguno de sus arquitectos, Charles Barry y Augustus Pugin, vivió para verlo terminado pero, a decir de todos, fue el trabajo de toda una vida y una saludable lección para los sucesores. El Senedd es solo un minúsculo edificio en comparación pero he logrado sobrevivir al proceso, aunque no sin pagar un precio, por mi parte, en dramatismo, placer y dolor.

Para los arquitectos, tener un organismo político como cliente constituye una experiencia realmente peculiar. Tenemos el placer de trabajar estrechamente y en confianza con todos nuestros clientes. Establecemos unas relaciones duraderas cuando los guiamos a lo largo de sus cometidos. Se trata de un enorme esfuerzo en equipo, por lo que éstas son fundamentales para el equipo. No obstante, en el Reino Unido, la arquitectura rara vez suele ser el pasatiempo de un político y hay pocos arquitectos que se dediquen a la política a tiempo completo. El periplo hasta entregar el Senedd fue testigo de las idas y venidas de numerosos funcionarios electos pero finalmente nos quedamos con un puñado de miembros de distintos partidos, junto con algunos cargos públicos expertos, cuyo punto en común era su amor por la arquitectura. Fue este equipo el que hizo realidad el Senedd. Es fundamental contar con un equipo de esta índole, apasionado por el urbanismo, para alcanzar el éxito en cualquier proyecto público.

Los arquitectos de los edificios públicos se suelen seleccionar a través de consultas abiertas; en el caso del Senedd, este proceso implicó una selección previa, seguida de una entrevista y, finalmente, un concurso limitado aunque remunerado. En este caso, solo buscaban el concepto. Cada competidor realizó luego una presentación ante un jurado de eminentes personalidades, presidido por el ex-primer ministro James Callaghan (Lord Callaghan of Cardiff) ayudado por asesores arquitectónicos. Esto permitió responder, en el momento, algunas preguntas y aclarar ciertas ideas. El proceso garantizó la igualdad de condiciones para la presentación del concepto más adecuado.

Junto con el programa preliminar para el Senedd se presentó un breve prólogo de Lord Callaghan que exponía las ambiciones de Gales como país y el modo en que esperaban que esto pudiera reflejarse en la nueva sede de gobierno:

« Este concurso ofrece a los profesionales de la arquitectura la oportunidad de expresar un concepto sobre la forma que debe adoptar una asamblea democrática que escucha y dirige a una pequeña nación democrática al alba del siguiente milenio… esperamos que se convierta en un símbolo visible, reconocido y respetado en todo el mundo, allí donde se utilice el nombre de Gales. »

Fue una declaración esclarecedora y conmovedora, y captó hábilmente cuál debía ser la inspiración de toda nueva sede de gobierno, independientemente de su tamaño.

Los arquitectos están acostumbrados a trabajar con limitaciones estrictas y, es cierto que a veces, cuantas más limitaciones, más ingeniosa se vuelve la solución y más arraigado en su contexto se torna el edificio propuesto. La presión de las expectativas del breve texto de Lord Callaghan, junto con una sede de relativamente escasas limitaciones físicas (un parque empresarial en las dársenas en desuso de Cardiff), provocó una situación inusual que, a primera vista, pudo haber favorecido los símbolos y los emblemas por encima del contexto y del emplazamiento.

La arquitectura, en particular la de los edificios gubernamentales, siempre tiene un contexto político y,

spricht, in Verbindung mit einem relativ unproblematischen Standort – ein Gewerbegebiet innerhalb der ungenutzten Docks von Cardiff – führten zu einer ungewöhnlichen Situation, die das Hauptaugenmerk vordergründig womöglich auf Symbole und Embleme statt auf den Kontext und das Umfeld gelenkt hätte.

Architektur – insbesondere jene von Regierungsgebäuden – weist stets einen politischen Kontext auf und im Fall des Senedd bestand keinerlei Zweifel daran, dass ein architektonischer Ausdruck geboten war, der zur Teilhabe einladen und über den Standort hinausreichen sollte – insbesondere in Anbetracht der unüberhörbaren öffentlichen Dezentralisierungsbestrebungen der walisischen Bevölkerung (die 1997 im Erfolg des walisischen Urnengangs zur Dezentralisierung zum Ausdruck kamen), und in Verbindung mit der anschließenden Auseinandersetzung über die Standortwahl für die neue Nationalversammlung. Die einzigartigen Bedingungen dieses für RSHP seit der Errichtung des Pariser Centre Pompidou im Jahr 1977 wohl mit dem breitesten öffentlichen Echo einhergehenden Bauvorhabens dienten als Katalysator für jenen Entwurf, der Wales einen unverwechselbaren Regierungssitz bescheren sollte.

Wir entschieden uns dafür, keine ästhetischen Metaphern, Symbole oder historischen Motive zu verwenden, – welche Architekten häufig als probates Mittel zur Beschwichtigung von Historizisten dienen und Ängstlichkeit über Authentizität stellen – sondern das Gebäude als strenge Antwort auf zwei fundamentale Fragen anzulegen: Wie müssten wir es am Standort errichten, um die Vorstellung einer grenzenlosen Verknüpfung von Bauwerk und Umland zu erwecken? Und wie müssten wir den öffentlichen und privaten Raum organisieren, um eine Teilnahme zwischen den Gewählten und den Wählenden anzuregen?

Unsere Antwort lag darin, den Blick über den zunächst profanen Standort hinaus und auf das Meer hin zu lenken, auf das übrige Land und die ferne Welt. Wir sahen den Standort als eine Verlängerung der Wasserfläche, nicht als Begrenzung derselben. Das Gebäudekonzept war dabei trügerisch einfach: ein simpler, fließender öffentlicher Raum, der sich von der Wasserkante zum Abgeordnetensaal hin erstreckt, und so eine weitläufige Schnittstelle der beiden Einheiten ermöglicht, um dergestalt öffentliches Engagement im politischen Raum zu fördern. So wäre das Gebäude in seinem Inneren dem Standort verhaftet und gleichzeitig am Äußeren orientiert. Ein über dem öffentlichen Raum schwebendes Gewölbe würde der Anlage eine vage Silhouette verleihen, über ihre Kleinheit inmitten der Nachbargebäude hinwegtäuschen und ihre Wirkung bis zur Wasserkante hin ausdehnen. Unserer Ansicht nach ein durchaus tragfähiges Konzept angesichts der vor uns liegenden Aufgabe, das sich schon recht bald als äußerst nützlich herausstellen sollte.

Ich erinnere mich noch an die erste Besprechung kurz nachdem sich RSHP (damals noch Richard Rogers Partnership) im Oktober 1998 im Wettbewerb durchgesetzt hatten. Eine Abordnung des damals noch mit der Koordinierung der Verwaltung von Wales betrauten Welsh Office kam in unser Büro in Hammersmith, im Westen Londons, und ließ anfragen, wann wir mit der Arbeit am Bauentwurf beginnen könnten. Höflich wiesen wir darauf hin, dass wir lediglich eine Idee entwickelt hatten, deren Ausarbeitung viele Monate dauern würde und in einer Zusammenarbeit mit ihnen bestehen müsste, um das Vorhaben in die Tat umzusetzen. Sie hatten nicht mit dieser Form der Zusammenarbeit gerechnet und konnten uns zu diesem Zeitpunkt noch nicht sagen, wer dafür zuständig sein würde, uns bei unserer Arbeit zu unterstützen. Ron Davies, der für Wales zuständige Minister, war soeben zurückgetreten und außerdem gingen sie wohl davon aus, dass wir unseren Entwurf bereits im Zuge des Wettbewerbs vollendet hätten.

Das Treffen unterstrich einen für uns zentralen und jedwedem Entwurf einer neuen Heimstätte für politische Führung zugrundeliegenden Faktor: Dass sich ein derartiges Unterfangen als weit emotionsgeladenere

quais désaffectés de Cardiff – ont contribué à générer une situation unique en son genre qui, à première vue, aurait pu favoriser le recours aux symboles et aux emblèmes sans égard à l'environnement ni au cadre.

L'architecture – surtout lorsqu'il s'agit de bâtiments publics – s'inscrit toujours dans un cadre politique et, concernant la Senedd, il était clair que, étant donné la forte aspiration publique du pays de Galles à la décentralisation (démontrée par le oui remporté lors du référendum sur le transfert des pouvoirs au pays de Galles en 1997), et l'argument qui a suivi selon lequel la ville accueillerait la nouvelle assemblée, le projet architectural devait apporter une réponse qui encourage la participation tout en incarnant une action qui dépasse le simple cadre du site. Ces conditions uniques présidant à la conception du bâtiment le plus officiel confiée à RSHP depuis le Centre Pompidou à Paris en 1977 ont finalement stimulé l'élaboration du projet dans le but de proposer un parlement distinctif du gouvernement gallois.

Nous avons donc pris le parti d'écarter les métaphores esthétiques, les symboles et autres motifs historiques – solution architecturale de facilité pour amadouer les historicistes et calmer les inquiétudes quant à l'authenticité du projet – pour définir le bâtiment comme une réponse limpide à deux questions fondamentales : comment insérer l'ouvrage dans le site de manière à suggérer l'idée que le lien entre l'édifice et son cadre ne souffre aucune limite ? Et comment organiser l'espace public et privé de manière à encourager la participation à la fois des élus et des électeurs publics ?

Nous avons donc cherché des pistes de réponse au delà du site à priori banal en se tournant vers l'environnement extérieur offert par la mer, les autres parties du pays et le monde qui l'entoure. Nous avons appréhendé le site comme une extension du plan d'eau et non comme sa limite. L'ouvrage s'est ainsi articulé autour d'un concept d'une simplicité apparente : un espace public d'un seul tenant à la circulation limpide qui s'étend du bord de l'eau jusqu'aux aménagements dédiés aux représentants élus, offrant un vaste lieu d'échanges avec les citoyens et encourageant la participation publique dans un espace politique. L'édifice serait ancré, de l'intérieur, à son site tout en regardant vers l'extérieur. Un auvent flottant au dessus de l'espace public conférerait à l'ensemble clos un contour fluctuant, dissimulant la taille relativement modeste de l'édifice par rapport aux ouvrages voisins, en étendant son influence jusqu'au bord de l'eau. Nous étions convaincus que notre concept résisterait aux aléas de l'aventure architecturale à venir. Et nos convictions ne tardèrent pas à se confirmer.

Je me souviens de notre première réunion de travail, peu de temps après que le cabinet RSHP (alors Richard Rogers Partnership) a été déclaré vainqueur du concours en octobre 1998. Une équipe du ministère des affaires galloises est arrivée dans notre bureau à Hammersmith, dans l'ouest de Londres, pour nous demander quand débuterait la conception du projet à construire. Ce à quoi nous avons poliment répondu que nous avions à peine défini l'idée générale et qu'il fallait envisager plusieurs mois de collaboration pour améliorer le concept avant qu'il ne prenne vie. Le ministère n'avait pas envisagé ce travail collaboratif dans sa feuille de route et était alors incapable de désigner quelqu'un apte à prendre des décisions pour nous aider à avancer. Le ministre pour le pays de Galles, Ron Davies, venait juste de démissionner de ses fonctions et, pour résumer, le ministère pensait que nous avions achevé la phase de conception pendant le concours.

Cette rencontre nous a permis de prendre en compte un facteur inhérent au travail de conception de tout nouveau siège de la direction politique, à savoir que ce type de client est plus souvent impliqué émotionnellement qu'un donneur d'ordres du secteur privé qui poursuit un objectif commercial, et bien plus que les autres promoteurs de programmes de construction publique, comme nous avons pu en faire l'expérience avec la conception des palais de justice de Bordeaux et d'Anvers. Un client privé qui n'a, dans l'ensemble, de compte à rendre qu'à lui même est libre de prendre des décisions que ne peuvent se permettre les dirigeants politiques.

en el caso del Senedd, estaba claro que, dada la pública proyección de la inclinación galesa por la devolución de poderes (demostrada en las urnas en el exitoso referéndum de devolución de poderes de Gales en 1997), junto con el posterior argumento de qué ciudad albergaría la nueva asamblea, la arquitectura iba a proporcionar una respuesta que fomentara la participación y representara algo más que el emplazamiento. Estas condiciones únicas para el edificio más público de RSHP desde el Centro Pompidou en París (1977) se convirtieron en el catalizador que iba a proporcionar una sede inconfundible para el Gobierno de Gales.

Decidimos no adoptar metáforas estéticas, ni símbolos ni motivos históricos (que constituyen a menudo una respuesta fácil del arquitecto para apaciguar a los historicistas y mitigar la preocupación por la autenticidad) sino definir el edificio como una respuesta estricta a dos preguntas fundamentales: ¿cómo podríamos colocarlo en el emplazamiento para que sugiriera que la conexión entre el edificio y la tierra no tenía límites? Y ¿cómo podríamos organizar el espacio público y privado para fomentar la participación entre los cargos electos y los electores públicos?

Nuestra respuesta fue mirar más allá de la prosaica posición inicial y salir al exterior, al mar, al resto del país y al mundo. Concebimos el emplazamiento como una extensión de la superficie del agua y no como su límite. El concepto del edificio era aparentemente sencillo: un único espacio público fluido, que se extendía desde el borde del agua hasta el espacio de los representantes del pueblo, lo que proporcionaba un amplio punto de contacto entre los dos y fomentaba el compromiso público en un espacio político. El edificio estaría anclado, internamente, en su emplazamiento, a la vez que estaría orientado hacia el exterior. Una cubierta flotante sobre el espacio público otorgaría un contorno impreciso al recinto, aumentando el pequeño tamaño del mismo entre sus vecinos y ampliando su influencia hasta el borde del agua. Un concepto sólido, creíamos, para el camino que nos esperaba. Y pronto se demostró lo importante que era.

Recuerdo la primera reunión que celebramos, justo después de anunciarse que RSHP (entonces, Richard Rogers Partnership) había sido el vencedor del concurso, en octubre de 1998. Un equipo del ministerio de Gales llegó a nuestro estudio en Hammersmith, en el oeste de Londres, y preguntó cuándo podíamos comenzar a desarrollar el diseño para la construcción. Sugerimos, amablemente, que solo habíamos concebido una idea y que tardaríamos meses en perfeccionarla, en colaboración con ellos, para que esta idea se hiciera realidad. No habían tenido en cuenta esta fase de colaboración en el proceso y no podían decir, en ese momento, quién podría tomar las decisiones para ayudarnos a lograrlo. El secretario de estado de Gales, Ron Davies, acababa de dimitir y, en resumen, pensaban que habíamos terminado nuestro diseño durante el concurso.

El encuentro resaltó para nosotros un factor clave inherente al diseño de cualquier sede nueva destinada a las autoridades políticas: que puede ser a menudo un asunto mucho más emocional que cualquier obra que se ejecute para un cliente del sector privado, con una orientación empresarial, y mucho más incluso que otros programas de construcción municipales, tal y como lo hemos experimentado en nuestros tribunales de Burdeos y Amberes. Un cliente privado, responsable, por lo general, solo ante sí mismo, tiene la libertad de tomar decisiones que la clase dirigente política no se puede permitir.

A pesar de esta creciente relación con el cliente, no obstante, resultó difícil extraer comentarios críticos que iniciaran un debate sobre el concepto. Sin otros precedentes que el deseo de que el edificio promoviera la cooperación en lugar de la disposición conflictiva del Palacio de Westminster (los partidos de la oposición se sientan enfrente), todo el equipo del cliente y de los asesores tenía poca o ninguna experiencia en la que inspirarse para hacer avanzar el diseño. Únicamente cuando una organización externa, que representaba a determinados grupos de

Aufgabe herausstellt als alle für geschäftsorientierte Privatkunden durchgeführten Projekte oder gar als zivile Baumaßnahmen, wie beispielsweise die von uns in Bordeaux oder Antwerpen errichteten Gerichtsgebäude. Ein Privatkunde – der zumeist nur sich selbst Rechenschaft schuldig ist – verfügt über eine Entscheidungsfreiheit, die dem politischen Establishment nicht gewährt wird.

Trotz intensivsten Kundenkontakts war es jedoch nicht einfach, kritische Aussagen zu erzeugen, die eine Konzeptkritik bewirkt hätten. Einzig und allein auf den Wunsch gestützt, dass das Gebäude als Fanal der Zusammenarbeit dienen und nicht wie der Westminster-Palast (mit den sich gegenübersitzenden gegnerischen Partein) die Konfrontation in den Fordergrund stellen sollte, mangelte es dem gesamten Auftraggeber- und Beratungsteam an der nötigen Erfahrung, einen derartigen Entwurf voranzubringen. Erst als eine externe Organisation, die eine Reihe von Behindertengruppen vertrat, während der öffentlichen Ausstellung zurecht ihre Bedenken hinsichtlich des Konzepts formulierte, kam es zu einer kritischen Diskussion, die den Entwurf schließlich in seine endgültige Form goss.

Bewilligt wurde der erneut vorgestellte Entwurf schließlich nach drei Jahren von Rhodri Morgan, dem dritten Ersten Minister von Wales. Nur ein einfaches, klares und tragfähiges Entwurfskonzept – für den Erfolg jeglichen Entwurfs eines öffentlichen Gebäudes meiner Ansicht nach ein unverzichtbares kritisches Charakteristikum – konnte diesen turbulenten Prozess überstehen; dass unsere ursprüngliche Idee überlebte, sehe ich als nachdrückliche Bejahung ihrer Tragfähigkeit. Die Gebäudeästhetik war die unmittelbare Konsequenz dieses Konzepts und erlaubte uns, den Entwurf ohne wiederholte subjektive Kritik an übertrieben symbolischen Entwürfen durch das Genehmigungsverfahren zu bringen. Der Senedd ist die von der Geschichte unbehauene Zukunft und gleichzeitig der Vorrang der eigenen Gegenwart.

Ich habe von physischen Zwängen gesprochen, die Entwürfe positiv beeinflussen, doch führen im öffentlichen Raum abgegebene Politikerzusagen häufig zu neuen Zwängen, die sowohl gesteigerte Ansprüche nach sich ziehen als auch vollkommenes Neuland für das Bauen an sich bedeuten können. Als Architekten sind wir uns über zwei Konstruktionskonstanten bewusst: Dass Bauregulierungen existieren, um die Allgemeingültigkeit von Standards zu gewährleisten, und, dass der freie Markt für Produkte und Dienstleistungen von der Gesetzgebung garantiert wird. Zusagen seitens der Politik können diese Konstanten stören, selbst wenn ihnen gute Absichten zugrunde liegen. Ein Bekenntnis zu einer vorbildlichen nachhaltigen Leistung und der unumstößliche Wunsch, ein walisisches Gebäude mit ausschließlich aus Wales stammenden Materialien zu errichten, gleich ob diese zur Verfügung stehen oder nicht, hatten Auswirkungen auf die zuvor festgelegten Budgetmittel. Ohne zugestandenen Handlungsspielraum ist auch ein noch so umsichtig geplantes Projekt vor störenden externen Einflüssen nicht gefeit; in unserem Fall hatten wir aufgrund der Anschläge vom 11. September mit noch nie dagewesenen Sicherheitsbedingungen zu kämpfen.

Bei der Entwicklung des Senedd mussten wir uns diesen Problemen stellen, hatten aber gleichzeitig nicht die Möglichkeit, über Kostenbilanz, Zeit oder Qualität zu diskutieren. Da die politischen Zusagen auf Grundlage sämtlicher Aspekte erfolgten, war keine einzige davon wirklich flexibel. Aufgrund unseres reichen Erfahrungsschatzes wussten wir, dass ein Bauprojekt ohne diese notwendige Flexibilität leicht aus den Fugen gerät. Hinsichtlich der Qualität lässt sich stets ein Einvernehmen finden, doch schwankt die Bedeutung der Kosten sowie der Dauer erheblich, hängen diese doch nicht nur von den Materialkosten ab sondern auch vom Beschaffungsprozess und der Art des Risikos.

Über sämtlichen zivilen Bauprojekten schwebten das Schreckgespenst einer öffentlichen Untersuchung und die ständig wiederholten Argumente hinsichtlich der Kosten; wäre es nicht besser, das „Geld in ein neues Krankenhaus

Malgré ce rapprochement privilégié avec le client, il a été difficile d'obtenir des remarques critiques afin d'instaurer un dialogue constructif autour du concept. À défaut d'autre instruction que le seul souhait de voir l'édifice promouvoir la coopération sans s'inscrire dans une logique de confrontation comme le suggère l'agencement du Palais de Westminster où les membres des partis rivaux se font face, l'équipe du client et des consultants n'avait que peu voire aucune expérience sur laquelle s'appuyer pour faire avancer les travaux de conception. Ce n'est que lorsqu'une organisation extérieure, représentant un certain nombre de groupes de personnes handicapées, a fait part à juste titre de ses inquiétudes concernant le concept alors exposé au public qu'un dialogue positif a pu se mettre en place et contribué à faire évoluer l'idée initiale jusqu'à sa forme définitive.

La représentation du concept a finalement été validée par Rhodri Morgan, troisième premier Ministre du pays de Galles depuis de nombreuses années. Seul un projet architectural simple, clair et fort, condition sine qua non à mon sens pour mener à bien la conception d'un bâtiment public, aurait pu survivre à un tel tumulte comme ce fut le cas pour notre proposition qui a remarquablement confirmé la puissance fédératrice de notre idée originale. L'esthétique générale de l'édifice a été directement dictée par ce concept, ce qui nous a permis de piloter le projet jusqu'à la phase d'approbation et de faire l'économie de nombreux débats subjectifs et répétitifs souvent cantonnés à des considérations trop symboliques. La Senedd se devait d'incarner l'avenir, sans tomber dans le passéisme, en puisant sa force dans le présent pour se forger ses propres références.

J'ai évoqué les contraintes physiques qui ont joué en faveur de la conception, mais dans l'arène publique, les promesses des hommes politiques exercent de nouvelles pressions qui, même si elles fixent des exigences plus fortes, peuvent faire basculer le travail de l'architecte en terrain inconnu. En tant qu'architectes, nous devons composer avec deux constantes en matière de construction : les règlementations en matière de construction garantissent le caractère universel des normes, et la législation garantit la libre commercialisation des produits et des services. Les promesses politiques, même si elles sont bien intentionnées, peuvent perturber l'application de ces constantes. L'engagement à produire un édifice exemplaire sur le plan du développement durable et la volonté inflexible de construire un bâtiment gallois uniquement avec des matériaux gallois, même indisponibles, ont compromis les dotations budgétaires décidées à l'avance. Les influences extérieures peuvent également désorganiser même les projets planifiés avec le plus grand soin si aucune marge de manœuvre n'est concédée. Dans notre cas, nous avons dû intégrer au projet des mesures de sécurité sans précédent après les attaques terroristes du onze septembre.

Lors de la conception de la Senedd, ces problématiques ont été traitées sans même la possibilité de débattre de l'équilibre entre coût, durée et qualité. Aucune concession n'a été envisagée dans la mesure où les politiques s'étaient engagés à tenir toutes leurs promesses. Nous savons d'expérience que sans une certaine flexibilité, n'importe quel projet de construction peut facilement échouer. Tout le monde s'accorde toujours sur la qualité, mais l'importance d'avancer rapidement et à moindre coût varie généralement en fonction du prix des matériaux, mais aussi des procédures de passation des marchés, ainsi que des types de risques encourus.

Aucun bâtiment civil n'échappe au regard critique du public, ni à l'argument récurrent du coût ; ne serait-il pas plus utile de « consacrer cet argent à la construction d'un nouvel hôpital plutôt qu'à une tribune de débats politiques onéreuse que nous n'avons jamais souhaitée ? ». Un bâtiment public offre une cible parfaite. Le moindre doute sur son coût final peut suffire à cristalliser tous les mécontentements.

discapacitados, mostró con razón su preocupación por el concepto, mientras se exhibía públicamente, se planteó un discurso crítico que hizo evolucionar finalmente la idea hacia su forma final.

El diseño presentado de nuevo recibió por fin la aprobación de Rhodri Morgan, el tercer primer ministro de Gales en tres años. Solo un concepto de diseño sencillo, claro y poderoso (una característica esencial, creo yo, para que cualquier diseño de edificio público sea un éxito) podría sobrevivir a este tumultuoso proceso. El hecho de que lo consiguiera no hizo sino demostrar el poder de la idea original. La estética del edificio fue una consecuencia directa de este concepto, lo que nos permitió desarrollarla a lo largo de todo el proceso de aprobación sin los reiterados debates subjetivos que surgen a menudo a partir de diseños excesivamente simbólicos. El Senedd representaba el futuro, sin la pátina de la historia y anclada en el presente, forjándose sus propias referencias.

He hablado de las limitaciones físicas que impulsan positivamente el diseño pero, en la plaza pública, las promesas de los políticos introducen nuevas limitaciones que, a la vez que elevan los estándares, pueden llevar al edificio a un territorio desconocido. Como arquitectos, somos conscientes de que existen dos constantes en la construcción: que las regulaciones sobre construcción existen para garantizar que los estándares sean universales y que la legislación garantiza un mercado libre para productos y servicios. Las promesas de los políticos, aunque fundadas en buenas intenciones, pueden desbaratar estas constantes. El compromiso con un rendimiento sostenible ejemplar y el deseo inflexible de construir un edificio galés a partir de materiales de Gales exclusivamente, aunque no estén disponibles, han complicado la dotación presupuestaria preestablecida. Las influencias externas pueden trastocar incluso el proyecto planificado con mayor cuidado si no hay espacio para maniobrar y, en nuestro caso, teníamos unas exigencias de seguridad sin precedentes que debíamos tener en cuenta después de los ataques terroristas del 11-S.

En el desarrollo del Senedd, nos enfrentamos a estos problemas sin la oportunidad de plantear un debate sobre el equilibrio de costes, plazos y calidad. No había aspectos flexibles, ya que los políticos habían hecho promesas sobre todos ellos. Sabemos, gracias a nuestra gran experiencia, que sin esta flexibilidad, un proyecto de construcción puede descarrilar fácilmente. Siempre se suele llegar a un acuerdo común sobre la calidad pero la importancia de la rapidez y el coste suele ser variable: viene determinada no solo por los costes de los materiales sino también por los procesos de contratación, así como por los tipos de riesgos.

Por encima de todos los proyectos municipales sobrevuela la mirada de la opinión pública, el manido argumento sobre los costes: no sería mejor «gastar el dinero en un nuevo hospital en lugar de en una costosa tertulia para políticos que nunca quisimos». Un edificio público es un objetivo fácil y cualquier duda sobre el coste final puede ser la crítica más fácil de todas.

Los edificios públicos y los debates sobre los costes se enmarcan siempre en torno a puntos negativos: gastos excesivos, presupuestos rebasados y plazos vencidos. Afortunadamente para el Senedd, el edificio del Parlamento de Escocia, en Edimburgo, realizado por EMBT y RMJM, se iba a entregar en un plazo de tiempo similar y, al comparar en tiempo real el coste de construcción por metro cuadrado, pudimos demostrar que el Senedd tenía una excelente relación calidad-precio. El debate político continuó, no obstante, y finalmente la constante presión provocó el estancamiento del proyecto.

Por su naturaleza, el número de edificios de parlamentos nuevos es escaso. Representa una oportunidad única en la carrera de un arquitecto y es un auténtico honor ser elegido para diseñarlo. En el sector de la construcción, los costes de edificación se suelen estimar, por lo general, mediante la evaluación comparativa continua con proyectos similares (esto permite al equipo de profesionales comprender

zu investieren, anstatt in eine teure Quasselbude für Abgeordnete, die wir von Anfang an nicht wollten".

Ein öffentliches Gebäude stellt ein leichtes Ziel dar und jegliche Unsicherheit hinsichtlich der abschließenden Kosten lässt sich im Handumdrehen in einen Treffer verwandeln.

Öffentliche Gebäude und die Auseinandersetzungen hinsichtlich der Kosten werden stets von Hiobsbotschaften begleitet: Kostenexplosion, Budgetkrise, Verzug. Erfreulicherweise für den Senedd wurde das Schottische Parlament in Edinburgh von EMBT und RMJM in vergleichbarer Frist fertiggestellt und wir konnten mithilfe eines Echtzeit-Vergleichs der Errichtungskosten pro Quadratmeter zeigen, dass der Senedd sein Geld wert war. Doch ging die politische Diskussion unverändert weiter und die fortwährende Belastung führte schließlich zu einem Projektstopp.

Neue Parlamentsgebäude werden von Natur aus nur sehr selten in Auftrag gegeben. Sie stellen ein einzigartiges Sprungbrett für Architekten dar und es ist eine große Ehre, für einen derartigen Entwurf ausgewählt zu werden. In der Bauwirtschaft werden Errichtungskosten für gewöhnlich durch einen Vergleich ähnlicher Projekte ermittelt – was es dem Expertenteam erlaubt, die gewünschte Qualität zu ermessen und diese mit den Kundenansprüchen abzugleichen – nur dass aufgrund ihrer relativen Seltenheit zum Zeitpunkt unseres Entwurfs für den Senedd in ganz Großbritannien kein einziges Parlamentsgebäude neu errichtet wurde. Zwei vergleichbare Entwürfe, das Schottische Parlament und das Hauptquartier der Greater London Authority (das Rathaus) von Foster + Partners, lagen zusammen mit dem Senedd noch auf dem Zeichenbrett. Ein vollumfassender Vergleich unseres Gebäudes war also schlicht und einfach unmöglich und die Alternative eines partiellen Abgleichs gestaltete sich aufgrund der exemplarischen Ansprüche des Senedd in Bezug auf Design, Nachhaltigkeit, Zugänglichkeit, Sicherheit und Material äußerst schwierig.

Bald nach dem Baubeginn wurde klar, dass der Beschaffungsprozess für die Nationalversammlung – aufgrund der schrittweisen Preisgabe von Informationen (einem eher bei knappen Fristen gewählten Verfahren) und mangels Sicherheit aufgrund eines Kostenvergleichs – das Risiko einer dramatischen Erhöhung des Baubudgets barg. Aufgrund komplizierter und vielfältiger Gründe wurde uns dieser Auftrag äußerst öffentlich entzogen. Wir haben auf die unkorrekte Beschaffungsmethode hingewiesen und dass diese unweigerlich die Überschreitung des Budgetrahmens nach sich ziehen würde, sollte sie fortgeführt werden. Die erneute Wiedervergabe an uns als die für den Entwurf und die Errichtung unter Vertrag genommenen Architekten bekräftigte unsere Position.

Die Nationalversammlung ermächtigte einen Sachverständigen, der über aktuelle Erfahrung im Bereich Projektabwicklung verfügte, und es verdankt sich diesem Beistand, dass der Fokus auf ihren Entscheidungsfindungsprozess gelegt, Emotionen außen vor gelassen und der Auslobungstext korrigiert werden konnte. Wir hatten dadurch genügend Zeit, um den vollständigen Gebäudeentwurf abzuschließen, und der Bauträger konnte einem Fixpreisvertrag zustimmen. Diese neue Vorgehensweise zeigte, dass hinsichtlich der Zeit ein wenig Flexibilität vorhanden war. Aufgrund dieser neuen Vereinbarung konnte das Bauvorhaben fortgesetzt und schließlich ohne weiteren Vorfall abgeschlossen werden.

Der Senedd war das erste Gebäudeprojekt, in dessen Errichtung RSHP involviert waren, welches in vollem Umfang auf Nachhaltigkeit setzte: graue Energie,

Or, les édifices publics et les débats autour de leur facture pour le contribuable ont souvent mauvaise presse : montants des dépenses qui explosent, dépassement de budget, hors budget. Heureusement pour la Senedd, le parlement écossais à Édimbourg conçu par EMBT et RMJM a été livré dans un délai similaire et, à comparaison égale du coût réel de construction par mètre carré, nous sommes parvenus à démontrer que la Senedd présentait un bon rapport qualité/prix. Le débat politique n'a pas cessé pour autant, les crispations constantes ayant fini par paralyser le projet.

Par définition, les nouveaux édifices parlementaires sont peu nombreux. Ils constituent une chance unique dans la carrière d'un architecte qui a l'immense honneur de s'en voir confier la conception. Dans le secteur de la construction, il est d'usage d'estimer en permanence les coûts par rapport à des projets de même ampleur. Cette méthode permet ainsi à l'équipe de professionnels de se faire une idée du niveau de qualité souhaité et de déterminer si ce niveau répond effectivement aux ambitions du client. Or, lorsque nous avons démarré le projet de la Senedd, il a été difficile de se référer à un projet similaire tant le nombre de parlements de construction récente reste rare au Royaume Uni. Les deux seuls projets comparables, à savoir l'édifice du Parlement écossais et le siège de l'Autorité du Grand Londres (l'Hôtel de ville) par Foster + Partners, étaient encore à l'étude, parallèlement à la Senedd. Il était donc tout simplement impossible de comparer le coût global du bâtiment. L'autre solution envisageable qui consiste à se référer à des éléments de coût comparables a en outre été compromise par les exigences d'édifier un bâtiment exemplaire en matière de durabilité, de développement durable, d'accessibilité, de sécurité et de matériaux respectueux de l'environnement.

Peu de temps après le début des travaux sur site, la procédure de passation des marchés de l'Assemblée, qui se fonde sur la communication échelonnée des informations, un processus normalement adopté lorsque la rapidité est essentielle en l'absence de référencement des coûts, a clairement menacé de faire considérablement augmenter le budget initial. Pour tout un ensemble de raisons complexes, le projet nous a été officiellement et publiquement retiré. Nous avions pourtant dénoncé la méthode de passation de marché et le risque qu'elle génère des surcoûts si elle était maintenue. Le fait que nous ayons été rappelés à nos fonctions d'architectes du projet aux termes d'un contrat « conception / construction » nous a finalement confortés dans notre position.

L'Assemblée a fini par mandater un agent ayant récemment travaillé à la livraison d'un projet. Ses recommandations ont permis de concentrer les efforts sur une prise de décision totalement désintéressée et sur la fixation d'un cap à tenir. Grâce aux délais ainsi accordés, nous avons pu terminer la conception complète du bâtiment et négocier avec le constructeur un contrat à prix fixe. Cette nouvelle façon de travailler a révélé une certaine souplesse en fin de compte. La nouvelle compréhension ainsi instaurée a permis de mener le projet jusqu'à son terme sans autre incident.

La Senedd a été le premier édifice pour lequel RSHP a adopté une approche durable de bout en bout du projet, qu'il s'agisse de son contenu énergétique, du choix des matériaux, des procédés de construction, des énergies consommées et de la pérennité du projet, autant de facteurs qui ont contribué, de manière exceptionnelle, à l'édification d'un ouvrage entièrement vitré et naturellement ventilé.

Le recours généreux à l'ardoise galloise s'est justifié en termes de contenu énergétique. Ce matériau a donc été préféré à d'autres sources, même si d'autres matériaux

la calidad deseada y si es coherente con las ambiciones de un cliente) pero su relativa singularidad suponía que no había edificios de parlamentos construidos recientemente en el Reino Unido cuando realizamos nuestro diseño para el Senedd. Los dos proyectos comparables, el edificio del Parlamento de Escocia y la sede de la Autoridad del Gran Londres (Ayuntamiento), de Foster + Partners, estaban en preparación a la vez que el Senedd. La evaluación comparativa de nuestro edificio en su conjunto era sencillamente imposible y la alternativa, la evaluación comparativa de elementos, se complicó debido a las exigencias ejemplares del Senedd sobre durabilidad, sostenibilidad, acceso, seguridad y materiales.

Nada más iniciar el proyecto in situ, quedó claro que el proceso de contratación de la Asamblea (basado en la publicación progresiva de información, un proceso que se adopta normalmente cuando la rapidez es esencial y sin la seguridad de los costes comparados) podría provocar un drástico incremento del presupuesto del edificio. Debido a toda una compleja serie de motivos, fuimos públicamente excluidos del proyecto. Sugerimos que el método de contratación presentaba ciertas deficiencias y que llevaría intrínsecamente a unos costes excesivos en caso de continuar con él. Al contratarnos de nuevo como arquitectos con un contrato de diseño y construcción, finalmente se afianzó nuestra posición.

La Asamblea facultó a un funcionario que contaba con experiencia reciente en la ejecución de proyectos y, gracias a su orientación, se dio protagonismo a la toma de decisiones, quitando emoción al asunto y estableciendo indicaciones. Esto nos dio tiempo para finalizar todo el diseño del edificio y permitió al constructor establecer un contrato con un precio fijo. Este nuevo proceso reveló que, a pesar de todo, había cierta flexibilidad: el tiempo. El nuevo acuerdo permitió al proyecto proseguir hasta su conclusión sin más incidentes.

El Senedd fue el primer edificio en el que se implicó RSHP que adoptó un planteamiento sostenible a lo largo de todo el proyecto, desde la energía incorporada, selección de materiales y prácticas de construcción, hasta la energía en uso y la durabilidad; factores que desembocaron, de forma excepcional, en un edificio con ventilación natural y simple acristalamiento.

El uso abundante de pizarra galesa estaba justificado en términos de energía incorporada sobre otras fuentes pero otros materiales no dieron la talla. Simplemente no había suficiente roble aprobado por el Consejo de Administración de Bosques de Gales para el tejado. Así que reservamos su uso para el mobiliario. Podíamos desviarnos radicalmente de los planes de construcción estándar del Gobierno del Reino Unido con ventanas perforadas en sólidas paredes y cortinas antiexplosión hacia un entorno más abierto al ofrecer una propuesta global de seguridad. Esta medida también ayudó a proporcionar el cambio más significativo en el marco físico: un parque empresarial convertido en un espacio público junto al agua, un patrimonio nacional para los habitantes de Gales.

¿Y cuál fue el resultado? Tardamos dos veces más en construirlo y costó el doble por metro cuadrado de lo previsto al principio pero, lo que es más importante, al final, la Oficina Nacional de Auditoría confirmó a la Asamblea que el Senedd ofrecía una buena relación calidad-precio.

El Palacio de Westminster y el Senedd tienen ambos su propia historia, con la diferencia de que la del Senedd está más fresca en nuestra memoria. Durante las fases finales de la accidentada construcción de Westminster, Pugin enloqueció tras la presentación de su diseño para la torre

Material- und Konstruktionsentscheidungen, Energieaufwand beim Betrieb und Gebrauchsdauer; ausnahmslos Faktoren, die erstaunlicherweise auf ein einfach verglastes, natürlich belüftetes Gebäude hindeuteten.

Die großzügige Verwendung walisischen Schiefers gegenüber anderen Materialien ergab sich aufgrund der grauen Energiebilanz, andere Materialien schafften es jedoch nicht in die engere Auswahl. Es gab einfach nicht genügend Eichenholz, das vom walisischen Forest Stewardship Council genehmigt worden war, um daraus das Dach zu errichten. Also beschränkten wir seine Verwendung auf die Einrichtung. Es gelang uns, den standardmäßigen Auslobungstext der britischen Regierung für gestanzte Fenster in Vollmauern weit hinter uns zu lassen, zugunsten einer offeneren Umgebung auf Stores zu verzichten und gleichzeitig ein umfassendes Sicherheitsangebot abzugeben. Dank dieser Vorgehensweise wurde auch die umfangreichste Veränderung des physischen Aufbaus möglich: ein zu einem öffentlichen Uferraum umgestaltetes Gewerbegebiet; ein nationales Monument für alle Waliserinnen und Waliser.

Das Ergebnis? Nun, die Errichtung dauerte doppelt so lange und war pro Quadratmeter doppelt so teuer als anfangs erwartet, doch bestätigte schließlich der britische Rechnungshof, dass der Senedd sein Geld absolut wert war.

Sowohl der Palace of Westminster als auch der Senedd erzählen beide ihre ganz eigenen Geschichten, nur dass die des Senedd sich noch frisch anfühlen. Im Endstadium der turbulenten Errichtung des Westminster-Palastes versank Pugin nach der Einreichung seines Entwurfs für den heute als Big Ben bekannten Glockenturm in Wahnsinn. Obwohl ich, anders als der arme Pugin, stets weit von einem Krankenhausaufenthalt in Bedlam entfernt war, habe ich doch mit den Vielschichtigkeiten eines Regierungsprojekts, die ihn möglicherweise dorthin geführt haben, Bekanntschaft gemacht. Die in diesem Buch gezeigten öffentlichen Gebäude erzählen ohne Ausnahme ähnliche Geschichten, die von der Entschlossenheit einer Vielzahl an Menschen erzählen, diese erstehen zu lassen. Ich empfinde große Bewunderung für all jene, die an deratigen Vorhaben mitwirken, und ihre besondere Toleranz und Hingabe an eine Arbeit, die unter derart strenger öffentlicher Kontrolle erfolgt.

n'ont pas été retenus. Ainsi, nous n'avions tout simplement pas assez de chênes ayant obtenu la certification galloise FSC (Forest Stewardship Council - Conseil de la bonne gestion forestière) pour le toit. Nous avons donc réservé ce matériau à la fabrication du mobilier. Nous avons pris d'importantes libertés par rapport au cahier des charges classique du gouvernement britannique qui préconise notamment des fenêtres poinçonnées encastrées dans des murs massifs et des rideaux anti-déflagration afin de concevoir un environnement plus ouvert tout en soumettant une proposition exhaustive en matière de sécurité. Grâce à cette approche, nous avons pu modifier en profondeur le cadre physique : une zone d'affaires transformée en un espace public en bord de mer, un bien national pour tout le peuple gallois.

Et pour quel résultat ? Et bien, la construction du projet a pris deux fois plus de temps qu'escompté et a coûté deux fois plus que le budget initialement prévu, mais au final, le plus gratifiant est que le National Audit Office (Cour des comptes britannique) a confirmé à l'Assemblée que la Senedd s'est avérée un investissement rentable.

Le Palais de Westminster, la Senedd, deux ouvrages avec leur propre histoire. Seule différence, la Senedd restera dans les esprits la construction la plus récente. Durant les dernières années de la construction mouvementée de Westminster, Pugin a sombré dans la folie après la soumission de son projet pour la tour horloge connue sous le nom de Big Ben. Si, contrairement à ce malheureux Pugin, je n'ai jamais été admis à Bedlam (hôpital psychiatrique de Londres), je peux dire aujourd'hui avoir pris la mesure des complexités que soulève un projet public, celles-là mêmes qui ont conduit mon prédécesseur à sa triste fin. Les bâtiments publics illustrés dans cet ouvrage raconteront sans doute des histoires semblables, toutes faisant honneur à la détermination de ceux qui ont contribué à leur donner forme. J'ai une grande admiration pour toutes ces personnes qui se sont impliquées, et pour leur dévouement particulier et la grande tolérance dont elles font preuve dans leur travail dont le fruit est toujours soumis aux critiques du public.

del reloj, conocida como Big Ben. Aunque yo, a diferencia del pobre Pugin, nunca ocupé una cama del hospital psiquiátrico de Bedlam, puedo entender las complejidades de un proyecto gubernamental que pudo llevarle hasta allí. Los edificios públicos que aparecen en este libro tendrán todos historias similares que contar, lo que demuestra la determinación de los que contribuyeron a materializar su existencia. Siento una gran admiración por todos los que participaron y su especial dedicación y tolerancia para trabajar bajo la atenta mirada de la opinión pública.

Austrian Parliament Building

Vienna, Austria
Theophil Hansen, 1883

In a fountain on the Ringstraße in central Vienna, a commanding 5.5-metre-tall sculpture of Pallas Athene, the goddess of wisdom, stands proudly before the magnificent façade of one of Europe's most storied parliaments. Originally the seat of legislature for the Habsburg Empire, it became the parliament for the First Austrian Republic in 1919. Austria declared itself a federal republic once again in 1945, after the Second World War, which saw half the building destroyed. Today the restored building houses the National and Federal Councils. Hansen's design, with clear parallels to his previous work on the Zappeion Hall in Athens, is in the neo-Greek tradition – a style specifically chosen to reflect the importance of democracy.

Gebieterisch und stolz ragt die 5,5 Meter hohe Statue der Pallas Athene, der Göttin der Weisheit, aus dem nach ihr benannten Brunnen auf, der unmittelbar vor der prachtvollen Fassade des österreichischen Parlaments an der Wiener Ringstraße und damit vor einem der wohl geschichtsträchtigsten Abgeordnetenhäuser Europas liegt. Im ursprünglich als Sitz des Reichsrats der Habsburgermonarchie dienenden Gebäude tagte seit 1919 das Parlament der ersten österreichischen Republik. Nach dem zweiten Weltkrieg, dem ein beachtlicher Teil des Gebäudes zum Opfer fiel, erklärte sich Österreich im Jahr 1945 ein weiteres Mal zur Bundesrepublik und noch heute beherbergt das wiedererstandene Hohe Haus sowohl den National- als auch den Bundesrat des Landes. Hansens Entwurf erinnert stark an sein zuvor in Athen errichtetes Zappeion und ist eindeutig und ganz bewusst neoklassizistisch geprägt, um dergestalt die Bedeutung der Demokratie zu untermauern.

Juchée sur une fontaine de la Ringstraße en plein centre de Vienne, une impressionnante sculpture de 5,5 mètres de haut de la Pallas Athéna, déesse de la sagesse, se dresse fièrement devant la somptueuse façade de l'un des parlements le plus prestigieux d'Europe. À l'origine siège du pouvoir législatif sous l'Empire des Habsbourg, le bâtiment devint le parlement de la première république autrichienne en 1919. Au lendemain de la Seconde Guerre mondiale, au cours de laquelle le bâtiment fut à moitié détruit, l'Autriche s'autoproclama de nouveau république fédérale en 1945. Aujourd'hui, l'édifice restauré abrite les chambres du Conseil national et du Conseil fédéral. La conception architecturale d'Hansen, qui rappelle clairement ses précédents travaux sur le Zappéion à Athènes, s'inscrit précisément choisi pour symboliser l'importance de la démocratie.

En una fuente de la Ringstraße, en el centro de Viena, una imponente escultura de 5,5 metros de altura de Palas Atenea, la diosa de la sabiduría, se yergue orgullosa ante la magnífica fachada de uno de los parlamentos más ilustres de Europa. Tras ser originalmente la sede legislativa del Imperio de los Habsburgo, se convirtió en el parlamento de la Primera República de Austria en 1919. Después de la Segunda Guerra Mundial, en la que la mitad del edificio quedó destruida, Austria se declaró república federal de nuevo en 1945. Actualmente, el edificio restaurado alberga los Consejos Nacional y Federal. El diseño de Hansen, que muestra un claro paralelismo con su anterior trabajo en el Zappeion de Atenas, sigue la tradición neogriega, estilo que se eligió expresamente para resaltar la importancia de la democracia.

Austrian Parliament Building, Vienna, Austria

Parliament House

Stockholm, Sweden
Aron Johansson, 1905

The complex of the Riksdag, partially situated on the island of Helgeandsholmen in the old town of Stockholm, was originally constructed to house both the parliament and the Swedish National Bank. The east wing, at the front, was to be the new home of the Riksdag, as reflected in its grand, neo-Baroque façade, complete with the national coat of arms and statue of Mother Svea, the allegorical representation of Sweden. The west wing, with its distinctive semicircular shape, was home to the National Bank until 1971, when it was repurposed as a new government assembly hall, and the wings are connected by two large arches that straddle a pedestrianised street below.

Der Gebäudekomplex des Riksdag, der teilweise auf der Insel Helgeands-holmen in der Stockholmer Altstadt liegt, war ursprünglich errichtet worden, um als Sitz sowohl des Parlaments als auch der Nationalbank Schwedens zu dienen. Der im Vordergrund liegende Ostflügel beherbergt den Riksdag, was durch seine gigantische Neobarock-Fassade verdeutlicht wird, die das Landeswappen sowie Mutter Svea zieren, die Nationalallegorie Schwedens. Im markanten, halbkreisförmigen Westflügel war die Nationalbank untergebracht, bis 1971 der neue Plenarsaal hierher verlegt wurde. Beide Flügel sind über zwei ausladende Bögen miteinander verbunden, die sich über eine zur Fußgängerzone umfunktionierte Straße spannen.

Le complexe du Riksdag, en partie situé
sur l'île d'Helgeandsholmen dans le
vieux centre-ville de Stockholm, a été
initialement construit pour héberger
à la fois le parlement et la banque
centrale de Suède. L'aile orientale,
à l'avant, a été déclarée nouveau
siège du Riksdag, à l'image de son
imposante façade néobaroque,
que viennent agrémenter les armoiries
nationales et la statue de Mère
Svea, figure allégorique de la Suède.
L'aile occidentale, avec sa forme
caractéristique en demi-sphère,
a hébergé la Banque nationale
jusqu'en 1971, année durant laquelle
l'aile fut recyclée en nouvelle salle
de l'Assemblée gouvernementale.
Les deux ailes sont reliées entre elles
par deux larges arches qui surplombent
une rue piétonne en contrebas.

La estructura del Riksdag, situada
parcialmente en la isla de Helgeands-
holmen en el casco antiguo de
Estocolmo, se construyó originalmente
para albergar tanto el parlamento como
el Banco Nacional de Suecia. El ala este,
al frente, se convirtió en la nueva sede
del Riksdag, tal como se refleja en su
grandiosa fachada neobarroca, adornada
con el escudo nacional y la estatua de la
Madre Svea, representación alegórica de
Suecia. El ala oeste, con su característica
forma semicircular, fue sede del
Banco Nacional hasta 1971, año en
que se replanteó como nueva asamblea
legislativa. Ambas alas están unidas por
dos amplios arcos que dan paso a una
calle peatonalizada en su parte inferior.

Parliament House, Stockholm, Sweden

Houses of Parliament

Cape Town, South Africa
Charles Freeman, Henry Greaves, 1885

In 1853 Queen Victoria granted permission for the establishment of a parliament in the Cape Colony, and construction on the Houses of Parliament began in 1875. It faced numerous upheavals – including the dismissal of the original architect – but was completed by 1885. The building's statuesque Corinthian porticos and impressive dome are fitting for one of the most dramatic political arenas in the world: it has been witness to, among other turbulent events, the Second Anglo-Boer War, the First and Second World Wars, the introduction of apartheid by the National Party, withdrawal from the Commonwealth in 1961, and the democratic elections of 1994, which began the gradual dissolution of apartheid.

1853 gab Königin Victoria ihre
Zustimmung zur Errichtung eines
Parlaments in der Kapkolonie,
woraufhin im Jahr 1875 der Grundstein
der Houses of Parliament gelegt wurde.
Obwohl der Bau zahlreiche Rückschläge
erlebte – darunter die Entlassung des
ursprünglichen Architekten – konnte
er im Jahr 1885 fertiggestellt werden.
Der statuenhafte korinthische
Portikus sowie die beeindruckende
Kuppel des Gebäudes sind diesem
hochdramatischen politischen
Schauplatz mehr als angemessen:
Neben anderen turbulenten Ereignissen
wurde das Land Zeuge der Burenkriege,
der beiden Weltkriege, der Verhängung
der Apartheid durch die Nationale
Partei, der Errungenschaften der 1961
erworbenen Unabhängigkeit und der
1994 abgehaltenen demokratischen
Wahlen, die zur schrittweisen Auflösung
des Apartheidregimes führten.

En 1853, la reine Victoria autorisa la colonie du Cap à bâtir un parlement. Les travaux de construction du parlement débutèrent en 1875. En dépit de nombreux bouleversements dont la démission de l'architecte à l'origine du projet, les travaux furent achevés en 1885. Les imposants portiques de style corinthien, de même que l'impressionnante coupole de l'édifice servent de décor à l'une des scènes politiques parmi les plus mouvementées du monde qui a été témoin, entre autres turbulences politiques, de la Guerre des Boers, de la Première et de la Seconde Guerre mondiale, de l'introduction de l'apartheid par le Parti national, de l'accession à l'indépendance en 1961, et des élections démocratiques en 1994, qui mirent progressivement fin à l'apartheid.

En 1853, la reina Victoria concedió un permiso para la creación de un parlamento en la colonia de El Cabo, pero la construcción de las cámaras del parlamento no se inició hasta 1875. Tras superar diversas turbulencias, incluida la destitución del arquitecto original, las obras finalizaron en 1885. Los esculturales pórticos corintios del edificio y la impresionante cúpula son dignos de uno de los marcos políticos más espectaculares del mundo: ha sido testigo, entre otros acontecimientos turbulentos, de la Guerra Anglo-Bóer, la Primera y la Segunda Guerras Mundiales, el establecimiento del apartheid por el Partido Nacional, la independencia lograda en 1961 y las elecciones democráticas celebradas en 1994, que marcaron el comienzo de la progresiva disolución del apartheid.

The colossal Hungarian Parliament Building was conceived in the years following the 1867 Austro-Hungarian Compromise, and was more than twenty years, 40 million bricks, and 40 kilogrammes of gold in the making. Situated on the banks of the Danube, construction on the neo-Gothic edifice, with its Renaissance Revival dome, began in 1885, and although incomplete the building was inaugurated in 1896 to commemorate the nation's millennium. Almost a century later, in October 1989, Mátyás Szűrös stood on one of the building's balconies, framed by its white sculptures and beneath its twenty-seven intricate spires, to declare the Third Hungarian Republic, signalling an end to four decades of communism.

Hungarian Parliament Building

Budapest, Hungary
Imre Steindl, 1904

Der Entwurf des gewaltigen ungarischen Parlamentsgebäudes entstammt der Zeit unmittelbar nach dem Österreichisch-Ungarischen Ausgleich von 1867 und verschlang bis zu seiner Fertigstellung über 20 Jahre Bauzeit, 40 Millionen Ziegel und 40 Kilogramm Gold. Die Errichtung des am Donauufer gelegenen neogothischen Baus mit seiner Neo-renaissance-Kuppel begann im Jahr 1885 und obwohl es elf Jahr später noch immer unvollendet war, wurde das Parlament 1896 anlässlich der ungarischen Milleniumsfeierlichkeiten eingeweiht. Beinahe ein Jahrhundert später, genauer gesagt im Oktober 1989, setzte Mátyás Szűrös auf einem der von weißen Skulpturen umrahmten Balkone unter den 27 aufwendig gestalteten Turmspitzen mit der Ausrufung der Dritten Ungarischen Republik vier Jahrzenten kommunistischer Herrschaft ein Ende.

Les plans de l'imposant édifice du Parlement hongrois ont été dessinés dans les années qui suivirent la signature du Compromis austro-hongrois en 1867. Son chantier a nécessité plus de vingt ans de travaux, 40 millions de briques, et 40 kilogrammes d'or. Situé sur les berges du Danube, les travaux de construction de l'édifice de style néo-gothique, avec son dôme de tradition néo-renaissance, débutèrent en 1885. Bien qu'inachevé, l'édifice fut inauguré en 1896 pour commémorer le millénaire de la nation. Près d'un siècle plus tard, en octobre 1989, depuis l'un des balcons du bâtiment, encadré de sculptures blanches, sous les vingt-sept flèches qui ornent le toit du parlement, Mátyás Szűrös proclama la troisième république hongroise, marquant la fin de quatre décennies de communisme.

El colosal edificio del Parlamento húngaro se diseñó en los años anteriores al Compromiso Austro-húngaro de 1867. Se tardó más de 20 años en su ejecución, que requirió 40 millones de ladrillos y 40 kilos de oro. Situado a orillas del Danubio, la construcción del edificio neogótico, con su cúpula neorrenacentista, comenzó en 1885 y en 1896, antes de acabarlo, se inauguró el edificio para celebrar los mil años de existencia de la nación. Casi un siglo después, en octubre de 1989, Mátyás Szűrös se presentó en uno de los balcones del edificio, enmarcado por esculturas blancas y bajo veintisiete intrincadas agujas, para proclamar la Tercera República Húngara, lo que marcó el fin de cuatro décadas de comunismo.

Old Royal Palace

Athens, Greece
Friedrich von Gärtner, 1843

The Old Royal Palace, originally built for King Otto, became home to the Hellenic Parliament in 1935. The palace is austere but imposing, Gärtner's neoclassical design combining functionality with elements of the Ancient Greek aesthetic. In 1924, Greece transitioned from monarchy to republic; the building was abandoned by the royal family and five years later the government decided to move the parliament and senate into the building. The palace was converted under the direction of Andreas Kriezis, and although the monarchy was reinstated in 1935, the parliament has remained there since.

Im ursprünglich für König Otto errichteten Alten Königsschloss wurde im Jahr 1935 das griechische Parlament untergebracht. Der strenge doch imposante, neoklassizistische Palast Gärtners verbindet Funktionalität mit Elementen altgriechischer Ästhetik. Als Griechenland 1924 von der Monarchie zur Republik überging, wurde das Gebäude von der königlichen Familie aufgegeben; fünf Jahre später entschied die Regierung, das Parlament sowie den Senat an diesen Ort zu verlegen. Der Palast wurde unter der Federführung Andreas Kriezis' umgebaut und obwohl das Land 1935 zur Monarchie zurückkehrte, verblieb das griechische Parlament in diesem Gebäude.

L'ancien Palais royal, à l'origine édifié pour le Roi Othon 1er de Grèce, est devenu le siège du parlement grec en 1935. Austère mais imposant, le palais construit par Gäertner dans un style néoclassique allie fonctionnalité et esthétique de la Grèce antique. En 1924, la Grèce a basculé de la monarchie à la république. Abandonné par la famille royale, le bâtiment finit par accueillir cinq ans plus tard le Parlement et le Sénat sur décision du gouvernement. Les travaux d'aménagement du palais furent confiés à Andreas Kriezis. Le Parlement y réside depuis, même pendant la restauration de la monarchie en 1935.

El antiguo Palacio Real, construido originalmente por el rey Otón, se convirtió en la sede del Parlamento Helénico en 1935. El diseño neoclásico de Gärtner para este palacio, austero e imponente a la vez, combina funcionalidad y elementos estéticos de la antigua Grecia. El año 1924 marcó la transición de Grecia de monarquía a república: la familia real abandonó el palacio y cinco años después el gobierno decidió trasladar el Parlamento y el Senado al nuevo edificio. El palacio se transformó bajo la dirección de Andreas Kriezis y, aunque la monarquía se restableció en 1935, el Parlamento siguió ocupando el mismo lugar.

Palace of Parliament

Bucharest, Romania
Anca Petrescu, 2005

Spanning a colossal 340,000 square metres, the leviathan Palace of Parliament – originally, and somewhat ironically, named Casa Poporului ('House of the People') – was built during one of the darkest periods of Romania's history: the reign of tyrannical Communist dictator Nicolae Ceauşescu. Construction began in 1983 with 20,000 labourers, work going on twenty-four hours per day, seven days a week, while standards of living plummeted to an all-time low. It was almost complete when the revolution began in 1989 and Ceauşescu was overthrown and executed. In time, the people have come to appreciate the palace, which today houses the parliament and the Museum of Contemporary Art – but more than half of it remains unoccupied.

Der 340.000 Quadratmeter
umspannende Kolossalbau des
Parlamentspalasts – der ursprünglich
und durchaus ironisch „Casa Poporului"
oder „Haus des Volkes" genannt wurde –
entstand im Laufe einer der wohl
dunkelsten Epochen der rumänischen
Geschichte: der Schreckensherrschaft
des kommunistischen Diktators
Nicolae Ceaușescu. 20.000 Arbeiter
schufteten ab 1983 rund um die Uhr
und sieben Tage die Woche an diesem
Bau, während der Lebensstandard
im Land auf ein nie zuvor gekanntes
Tief abrutschte. Als das Gebäude
1989 beinahe vollendet war, brach die
Revolution aus und wurde Ceaușescu
gestürtzt und hingerichtet. Mit der
Zeit wuchs der Parlamentspalast den
Menschen in Rumänien dennoch ans
Herz und heute beherbergt er neben
dem Parlament auch das Nationale
Museum für Gegenwartskunst – wenn
auch die Hälfte der Flächen leersteht.

Occupant une incroyable surface de 340 000 mètres carrés, le colossal Palais du Parlement, à l'origine appelé, ironie du sort, la Casa Poporului (la « Maison du peuple »), a été construit durant la période la plus sombre de l'histoire roumaine, sous le règne du dictateur communiste tyrannique Nicolae Ceaușescu. Les travaux de construction débutèrent en 1983 et mobilisèrent 20 000 ouvriers à raison de vingt-quatre heures de travail par jour, sept jours sur sept, alors que les conditions de vie étaient à leur niveau le plus bas. L'édifice était quasiment achevé en 1989 lorsque la révolution éclata conduisant au renversement et à l'exécution de Ceaușescu. Au fil du temps, le peuple roumain a appris à apprécier le palais qui accueille aujourd'hui le Parlement et le Musée d'art contemporain. Plus de la moitié de l'édifice reste cependant inoccupée.

Con una superficie colosal de 340.000 metros cuadrados, el Palacio del Parlamento, un auténtico leviatán, llamado originalmente, de forma algo irónica, Casa Poporului («Casa del Pueblo») se edificó durante uno de los períodos más sombríos de la historia de Rumanía: el gobierno del tiránico dictador comunista Nicolae Ceaușescu. Las obras, iniciadas en 1983 con la colaboración de 20.000 obreros, se llevaron a cabo 24 horas al día, siete días a la semana, mientras el nivel de vida se desplomaba a mínimos históricos. In 1989, estando prácticamente finalizado, comenzó la revolución que derrocó y ejecutó a Ceaușescu. Con el tiempo, se ha llegado a apreciar más el palacio, que alberga actualmente el Parlamento y el Museo de Arte Contemporáneo, pero más de la mitad del edificio sigue desocupada.

The Union Buildings are the official seat of the South African government and the offices of the president. Pretoria became the administrative capital of South Africa in 1910, with the formation of the Union of South Africa, and the cornerstone of the building was laid later that year. Built from indigenous light sandstone, the complex forms a semicircle with two wings, which represents the union of a once-divided people. Union Buildings is an iconic landmark for South Africa; it was here, in 1994, that Nelson Mandela was inaugurated as the first democratically elected president, and in 2013 a 9-metre-high bronze statue was unveiled on the grounds in his memory.

Die Union Buildings sind der offizielle Sitz der Regierung Südafrikas und beherbergen weiters das Büro des Staatspräsidenten. Mit der Gründung der Südafrikanischen Union wurde Pretoria 1910 zur Verwaltungshauptstadt des Landes und die Grundsteinlegung für das Parlamentsgebäude erfolgte noch im selben Jahr. Die aus einheimischem hellem Sandstein erbaute Anlage bildet einen zweiflügeligen Halbkreis, der die Vereinigung eines zuvor geteilten Volkes symbolisiert und ein einzigartiges Wahrzeichen Südafrikas darstellt. An diesem Ort fand im Jahr 1994 die Angelobung Nelson Mandelas zum ersten demokratisch gewählten Präsidenten des Landes statt und wurde 2013 zu seinem Gedenken eine neun Meter hohe Bronzestatue enthüllt.

Union Buildings

Pretoria, South Africa
Herbert Baker, 1913

Les Union Buildings (Bâtiments
de l'Union) sont le siège officiel
du gouvernement sud-africain et
accueillent les bureaux du président.
Pretoria est devenue la capitale
administrative de l'Afrique du Sud
en 1910, avec la formation de l'Union
d'Afrique du Sud. La première pierre
de l'édifice fut posée la même année.
Construit à partir de grès clair de
la région, le complexe forme une
demi-sphère flanquée de deux ailes
et symbolise l'union d'un peuple
autrefois divisé. Union Buildings
est un haut lieu emblématique
de l'Afrique du Sud ; c'est ici que
Nelson Mandela fut officiellement
intronisé premier président élu
démocratiquement en 1994, et qu'une
statue de bronze de 9 mètres de haut
fut inaugurée en 2013 en sa mémoire.

En los Edificios de la Unión se encuentran la sede oficial del Gobierno de Sudáfrica y el despacho del presidente. En 1910, gracias a la formación de la Unión Sudafricana, Pretoria se convirtió en la capital administrativa del país. La primera piedra del edificio se colocó ese mismo año unos meses más tarde. El conjunto de edificios, construido en una piedra arenisca ligera autóctona, forma un semicírculo con dos alas, que representa la unión de un pueblo antaño dividido. Los Edificios de la Unión constituyen un monumento emblemático para Sudáfrica: en 1994, fue aquí donde Nelson Mandela fue investido presidente, el primero por elección democrática, y, en 2013, se erigió en los jardines una estatua de bronce de nueve metros en su memoria.

The Knesset Building

Jerusalem, Israel
Ossip Klarwein, 1966

The Knesset Building reflects the values of a complex government; behind three iron gates stands the austere rectangular complex, each side adorned with ten columns, in a modern, defensive interpretation of the Parthenon. Situated on land leased from the Greek Orthodox Patriarchate of Jerusalem, the Knesset Building was constructed using funds donated by James A. de Rothschild. Inside, visitors to the Knesset can watch debates in the main Plenary Hall and view the Chagall Hall, a reception area decorated by renowned artist Marc Chagall, whose colourful tapestries and mosaics depict the journey of the Jewish people from Biblical times to the founding of the modern state of Israel.

Das Knesset-Gebäude spiegelt die Werte einer vielschichtigen Staatsgewalt: hinter drei ehernen Toren erhebt sich ein strenger rechteckiger Komplex, dessen Seiten jeweils zehn Säulen schmücken und das Ensemble als defensive Variante des Parthenon erscheinen lassen. Die Knesset liegt auf einem Stück Land, das vom griechisch-orthodoxen Patriarchat von Jerusalem verliehenen wurde, und verdankt sich der finanziellen Unterstützung des Baron-James-de-Rothschild-Fonds. Im Gebäudeinneren haben Besucher die Möglichkeit, im Hauptplenarsaal politische Debatten zu verfolgen oder den Chagall-Saal zu bewundern, der als Empfangsbereich dient und vom renommierten Künstler Marc Chagall gestaltet wurde. Anhand farbenprächtiger Tapisserien und Mosaike wird hier die Reise des jüdischen Volks von der biblischen Vorzeit bis zur Gründung des modernen Staates Israel geschildert.

La Knesset incarne les valeurs d'un gouvernement complexe ; trois portails en fer s'ouvrent sur l'austère complexe rectangulaire, dont chaque côté est orné de dix colonnes, dans une réécriture moderne et défensive du Parthénon. Située sur un terrain loué au Patriarcat orthodoxe grec de Jérusalem, la Knesset a été construite grâce aux fonds levés par James A. de Rothschild. À l'intérieur, les visiteurs peuvent assister aux débats dans la principale salle des séances plénières et admirer le Hall Chagall, salon de réception décoré par l'artiste de renom Marc Chagall, dont les tapisseries et les mosaïques chatoyantes retracent l'histoire du peuple juif depuis l'époque biblique jusqu'à la création de l'état moderne d'Israël.

El edificio de la Knéset refleja los valores de un gobierno complejo; detrás de tres puertas de hierro se encuentra un conjunto rectangular austero, cada uno de cuyos lados está adornado por diez columnas, en una interpretación moderna y defensiva del Partenón. Situado en una tierra arrendada al patriarca griego ortodoxo de Jerusalén, el edificio de la Knéset se construyó gracias a unos fondos donados por James A. de Rothschild. En el interior, los visitantes de la Knéset pueden asistir a debates en el Salón de Plenos principal y ver el Salón Chagall, una zona de recepción decorada por el célebre artista Marc Chagall, cuyos coloridos tapices y mosaicos describen el recorrido histórico del pueblo judío desde los tiempos bíblicos hasta la fundación del moderno Estado de Israel.

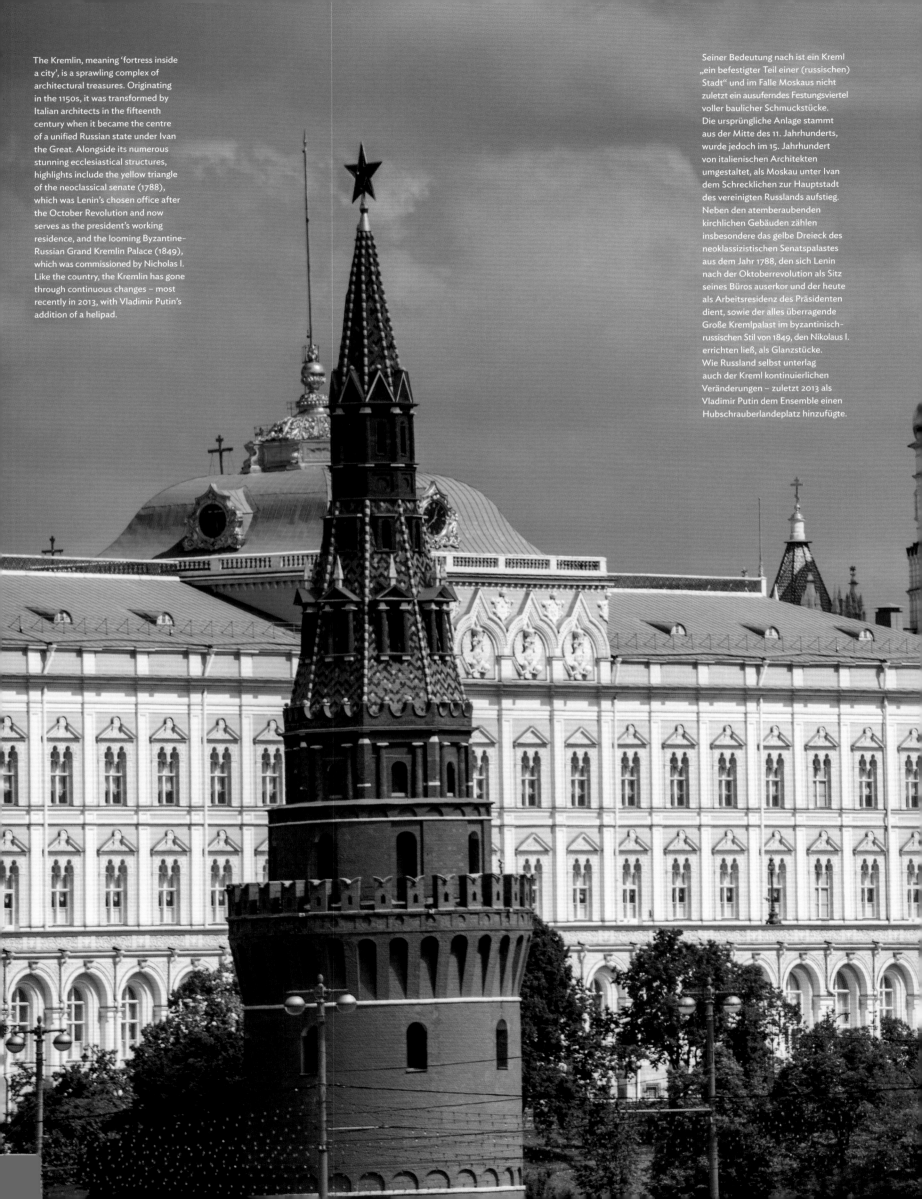

The Kremlin, meaning 'fortress inside a city', is a sprawling complex of architectural treasures. Originating in the 1150s, it was transformed by Italian architects in the fifteenth century when it became the centre of a unified Russian state under Ivan the Great. Alongside its numerous stunning ecclesiastical structures, highlights include the yellow triangle of the neoclassical senate (1788), which was Lenin's chosen office after the October Revolution and now serves as the president's working residence, and the looming Byzantine-Russian Grand Kremlin Palace (1849), which was commissioned by Nicholas I. Like the country, the Kremlin has gone through continuous changes – most recently in 2013, with Vladimir Putin's addition of a helipad.

Seiner Bedeutung nach ist ein Kreml „ein befestigter Teil einer (russischen) Stadt" und im Falle Moskaus nicht zuletzt ein ausuferndes Festungsviertel voller baulicher Schmuckstücke. Die ursprüngliche Anlage stammt aus der Mitte des 11. Jahrhunderts, wurde jedoch im 15. Jahrhundert von italienischen Architekten umgestaltet, als Moskau unter Ivan dem Schrecklichen zur Hauptstadt des vereinigten Russlands aufstieg. Neben den atemberaubenden kirchlichen Gebäuden zählen insbesondere das gelbe Dreieck des neoklassizistischen Senatspalastes aus dem Jahr 1788, den sich Lenin nach der Oktoberrevolution als Sitz seines Büros auserkor und der heute als Arbeitsresidenz des Präsidenten dient, sowie der alles überragende Große Kremlpalast im byzantinisch-russischen Stil von 1849, den Nikolaus I. errichten ließ, als Glanzstücke. Wie Russland selbst unterlag auch der Kreml kontinuierlichen Veränderungen – zuletzt 2013 als Vladimir Putin dem Ensemble einen Hubschrauberlandeplatz hinzufügte.

Moscow Kremlin

Moscow, Russia
1495

Le Kremlin, qui signifie en russe « forteresse urbaine », désigne un vaste complexe de bijoux architecturaux. Apparu dans les années 1150, le Kremlin a été transformé par des architectes italiens au quinzième siècle lorsque l'édifice fut proclamé centre de l'état russe unifié sous Ivan le Grand. Outre ses nombreux ouvrages sacrés époustouflants, le Kremlin se distingue également par le triangle jaune que forme le Sénat au style néoclassique (1788), siège du gouvernement proclamé par Lénine après la Révolution d'octobre, qui abrite aujourd'hui la résidence de travail du Président, ainsi que par l'imposant Grand Palais du Kremlin d'influence byzantine et russe (1849), commandé par Nicolas Ier. À l'instar du pays, le Kremlin ne cesse de se transformer, le dernier ajout en date étant une plate-forme d'atterrissage pour hélicoptère commandée par Vladimir Poutine en 2013.

El Kremlin, que significa «fortaleza dentro de una ciudad», está constituido por un amplio conjunto de tesoros arquitectónicos. Construido originalmente en la década de 1150, en el siglo XV se convirtió, gracias a la colaboración de arquitectos italianos, en el centro de un estado ruso unificado durante el reinado de Iván el Grande. Además de sus numerosas y sorprendentes estructuras eclesiásticas, los elementos más destacados incluyen el triángulo amarillo del Senado de estilo neoclásico (1788), que fue la sede de gobierno elegida por Lenin después de la Revolución de Octubre y que sirve ahora como residencia de trabajo del presidente, y el imponente Palacio del Gran Kremlin de gusto ruso-bizantino (1849), realizado por orden de Nicolás I. Al igual que el país, el Kremlin ha sufrido numerosos cambios, el más reciente en 2013, con la construcción del helipuerto de Vladímir Putin.

The African Union, which includes all states on the continent except Morocco, was established in 2001 with numerous aims, among them to achieve greater solidarity between Africans, to protect African interests internationally, and to promote peace, democracy and human rights. A new twenty-storey, 52,000-square-metre complex for the Union was inaugurated in 2012, having been funded and built by the Chinese government to demonstrate their support for the future of Africa. Its tower measures 99.9 metres, symbolising the signing of the Sirte Declaration on 9 September 1999, the first step towards the foundation of the Union, and outside a golden statue celebrates Kwame Nkrumah, the founding father of Pan-Africanism.

African Union Conference Center and Office Complex

Addis Ababa, Ethiopia
Ren Lizhi, 2012

Die Afrikanische Union, welcher
außer Marokko sämtliche Staaten
des Kontinents angehören, wurde im
Jahr 2001 gegründet, um zahlreiche
Ziele zu verfolgen, darunter die
Verbesserung der Solidarität unter
Afrikanern, die weltweite Wahrung
afrikanischer Interessen und nicht
zuletzt die Förderung des Friedens,
der Demokratie und der Menschen-
rechte. Der neue, zwölfgeschossige
und 52.000 Quadratmeter große
Unionskomplex, der von der
chinesischen Regierung als Zeichen
ihrer Unterstützung Afrikas auf
dem Weg in die Zukunft finanziert
und errichtet worden war, wurde
im Jahr 2012 feierlich eingeweiht.
Die Gebäudehöhe von exakt 99,9
Metern steht symbolisch für die
Unterzeichnung der Sirte-Deklaration
am 9. September 1999, die schließlich
zur Gründung der Union führen
sollte. Vor dem Gebäude erhebt
sich die goldene Statue Kwame
Nkrumahs, des wohl berühmtesten
Verfechters des Panafrikanismus.

L'Union africaine, qui regroupe tous les états du continent à l'exception du Maroc, a été créée en 2001 pour répondre à divers objectifs, comme notamment instaurer une plus grande solidarité entre Africains, protéger les intérêts africains à l'international et promouvoir la paix, la démocratie et les droits de l'homme. L'Union a inauguré en 2012 un nouveau complexe de 20 étages sur 52 000 mètres carrés, financé et construit par le gouvernement chinois désireux d'accompagner l'Afrique dans ses projets d'avenir. Cette tour de 99,9 mètres de haut symbolise la signature de la Déclaration de Syrte le 9 septembre 1999, première étape de la fondation de l'Union. Dehors, une statue en or a été érigée en l'honneur de Kwame Nkrumah, père fondateur du panafricanisme.

La Unión Africana, constituida por todos los estados del continente excepto Marruecos, se fundó en 2001 con numerosos objetivos que cumplir, entre ellos, lograr una mayor solidaridad entre los africanos, proteger los intereses de África a nivel internacional y promover la paz, la democracia y los derechos humanos. En 2012, la Unión inauguró un nuevo complejo de veinte plantas y 52.000 metros cuadrados, financiado y construido por el Gobierno chino, como prueba de su apuesta por el futuro de África. Su torre, con una altura de 99,9 metros, simboliza la firma de la Declaración de Sirte el 9 de septiembre de 1999, el primer paso que se dio para la creación de la Unión. En el exterior, una estatua dorada rinde homenaje a Kwame Nkrumah, el fundador del panafricanismo.

Georgian Parliament Building

Kutaisi, Georgia
Mamoru Kawaguchi & Kenichi Kawaguchi, 2012

Since it gained independence from the Soviet Union in 1991, Georgia has gone to great lengths to distance itself from communism and establish its own aesthetic. One major step was to relocate the parliament from its Soviet-era building in Tbilisi to the second city of Kutaisi. This new building could not be more different from its predecessor, with its modern, clean lines and its 40-metre-high glass dome, symbolising openness and transparency. The move was met with much criticism – regarding the cost, its distance from the capital, and the decision to build on the site of a Second World War memorial – but the finished complex reflects a government that is looking to the future.

Seit der Unabhängigkeit des Landes von der Sowjetunion im Jahr 1991 hat Georgien große Anstrengungen unternommen, um sich vom Kommunismus zu distanzieren und eine eigen Ästhetik zu entwickeln. Ein bedeutender Schritt auf diesem Weg war die Verlegung des Parlaments von seinem aus der Sowjetzeit stammenden Tifliser Standort in die zweitgrößte Stadt Kutaissi. Mit seinen modernen, schlichten Linien und seiner 40 Meter hohen Glaskuppel, die Offenheit und Transparenz symbolisiert, könnte sich dieses neue Gebäude kaum deutlicher von seinem Vorgänger unterscheiden. Wiewohl diese Wahl äußerst kritisch aufgenommen wurde – moniert wurden die Kosten, die große Entfernung zur Hauptstadt sowie die Entscheidung, auf einer Gedenkstätte aus dem zweiten Weltkrieg zu bauen – steht die vollendete Anlage doch für eine zukunftsorientierte Regierung.

Depuis qu'elle a acquis son indépendance de l'Union soviétique en 1991, la Géorgie n'a eu de cesse que de prendre ses distances avec le communisme et d'établir ses propres règles esthétiques. Une étape décisive de ce processus a été marquée par le déménagement du parlement de son bâtiment de l'ère soviétique à Tbilissi vers la deuxième ville du pays, Koutaïssi. Le nouvel édifice ne pouvait pas être plus différent que son prédécesseur, avec ses lignes modernes et propres et son dôme vitré de 40 mètres de haut, symbolisant l'ouverture et la transparence. Largement critiqué en raison de son coût, de l'éloignement avec la capitale, et de la décision de bâtir sur le site d'un mémorial dédié à la Seconde Guerre mondiale, le complexe aujourd'hui achevé incarne un gouvernement résolument tourné vers l'avenir.

Desde que logró independizarse de la Unión Soviética en 1991, Georgia ha recorrido un largo trecho para distanciarse del comunismo y establecer sus propias reglas estéticas. Un avance importante fue el traslado del parlamento desde un edificio típicamente soviético, en Tbilisi, a la segunda ciudad más grande del país, Kutaisi. Esta nueva construcción no podía ser más distinta de su predecesora, gracias a unas líneas modernas y nítidas, y una cúpula de cristal de 40 metros, símbolo de apertura y transparencia. El traslado se enfrentó a innumerables críticas, debido al coste, la distancia de la capital y la decisión de construir en el emplazamiento de un monumento a la Segunda Guerra Mundial, pero el conjunto acabado representa un gobierno que dirige su mirada hacia el futuro.

Government House of Baku

Baku, Azerbaijan
Lev Rudnev & V.O. Munts, 1952

Azerbaijan lies in an enviable position between Europe and Asia, in an area rich with natural resources. Thus, for centuries, empires have fought for its occupation, including the Greeks, the Romans, the Mongols, and the Russians. It was under Russian control, in 1934, that plans to build Government House (then 'Baku Soviet Palace') were announced. Construction began two years later, and lasted until 1952. This colossal Stalinist edifice was designed to accommodate 5,500 people and it is the most popular tourist attraction in the country. Since 1991, when Azerbaijan gained independence, it has housed numerous state ministries.

Aserbaidschan bildet eine vielbeneidete und an natürlichen Ressourcen reiche Schnittstelle zwischen Europa und Asien, weshalb im Laufe der Geschichte immer neue Eroberer danach trachteten, dieses Land zu unterwerfen, darunter Griechen, Römer, Mongolen und Russen. Unter russischer Herrschaft erfolgte schließlich im Jahr 1934 auch die Errichtung eines Regierungsgebäudes, des damaligen Sowjetpalastes von Baku. Die Grundsteinlegung erfolgte zwei Jahre später und zog sich bis 1952 hin. Bis zu 5500 Menschen finden in diesem gigantischen stalinistischen Gebäude Platz, bei dem es sich außerdem um die beliebteste Touristenattraktion des Landes handelt. Seit der Unabhängigkeit Aserbaidschans im Jahr 1991 waren zahlreiche Staatsministerien hier untergebracht.

Entre Europe et Asie, l'Azerbaïdjan
jouit d'une position privilégiée dans
une région riche en ressources
naturelles. Ainsi, pendant des siècles,
de nombreux empires, parmi lesquels
les Grecs, les Romains, les Mongols
et les Russes, se sont battus pour
en obtenir le contrôle. Le projet de
construire le Parlement (appelé alors
« Palais soviétique de Bakou ») fut
annoncé en 1934, sous l'occupation
russe. Les travaux débutèrent deux ans
plus tard pour finalement s'achever
en 1952. Cet imposant édifice
stalinien fut dessiné pour accueillir
5 500 personnes. C'est aujourd'hui
l'attraction touristique la plus visitée
du pays. Depuis 1991, année de
l'indépendance du pays, le bâtiment a
hébergé de nombreux ministres d'état.

Azerbaiyán ocupa una posición envidiable entre Europa y Asia, en una zona con numerosos recursos naturales. Durante siglos, diversos imperios lucharon por su ocupación, incluidos los griegos, romanos, mogoles y rusos. En 1934, bajo el control ruso, se anunció el plan para la construcción de la sede del gobierno (en aquella época era conocido como «Palacio Soviético de Bakú»). La construcción, que comenzó dos años después, duró hasta 1952. Este colosal edificio estalinista, diseñado para acoger a 5.500 personas, constituye la atracción turística más popular del país. Desde 1991, año de la independencia de Azerbaiyán, ha sido la sede de numerosos ministerios estatales.

In 1991, Kazakhstan became the
last Soviet Republic to declare
independence. Three years later
it was confirmed that the capital
would be changed from Almaty to the
planned city of Astana, providing the
opportunity to supplant the prevalent
Soviet architecture with modern
structures that incorporated traditional
Kazakh motifs. This move was carried
out in 1998, and the parliament
building, comprised of four blocks,
is a quintessential representation
of President Nazarbayev's vision.
It is the core building in the new
government district, already a sparkling
development of white, blue and gold,
which is due for completion in 2030.

Als letzte der ehemaligen Sowjet-
republiken erklärte Kasachstan
1991 seine Unabhängigkeit.
Gerade einmal drei Jahre später
wurde beschlossen, die Hauptstadt
von Almaty in die Reißbrettstadt
Astana zu verlegen, und diese
Gelegenheit gleichzeitg dafür
zu nutzen, die vorherrschende
Sowjetarchitektur durch eine
Verbindung aus modernen Strukturen
und traditionellen kasachischen
Motiven zu ersetzen. Die Umsetzung
erfolgte 1998 und das aus vier Blöcken
bestehende Parlamentsgebäude
bezeugt wie kein zweites Präsident
Nasarbajews Vision. Es ist das
zentrale Gebäude innerhalb des
neuen Regierungsviertels und
steht bereits vor der geplanten
Fertigstellung im Jahr 2030 für
die architektonische Entfaltung
der Farben Weiß, Blau und Gold.

Mazhilis Parliament Building

Astana, Kazakhstan
Ahsel Group, 2004

En 1991, le Kazakhstan devient la dernière république soviétique à déclarer son indépendance. Trois ans plus tard, la décision d'établir la capitale jusqu'alors située à Almaty dans la nouvelle ville planifiée d'Astana est confirmée, offrant ainsi l'opportunité de remplacer l'architecture soviétique dominante par des structures modernes qui intègrent les motifs traditionnels kazakhs. Les travaux débutèrent en 1998, et le bâtiment du Parlement, composé de quatre immeubles, incarne à lui tout seul la vision du président Nazarbaïev. Il s'inscrit au cœur du nouveau complexe gouvernemental, qui offre déjà un tableau chatoyant de blanc, de bleu et d'or, et devrait être achevé en 2030.

En 1991, Kazajistán se convirtió en la última república soviética en proclamar su independencia. Tres años después se confirmó que la capital se trasladaría de Almatý a la ciudad planificada de Astaná, lo que proporcionó la oportunidad de sustituir la arquitectura soviética predominante por modernas arquitecturas con motivos kazajos tradicionales. El traslado se llevó a cabo en 1998. El edificio del Parlamento, con sus cuatro bloques, constituye la máxima representación de la visión del presidente Nazarbayev. Elemento principal del nuevo barrio del gobierno, y con una finalización prevista para el año 2030, exhibe una brillante variación de blancos, azules y dorados.

The complex of the Indian Parliament, enclosed by a red sandstone wall, was constructed over six years under the direction of Lutyens and Baker, who were responsible for the planning of the colonial capital city of New Delhi. The parliament buildings pay respect to Indian architectural traditions, and the plan of the circular Central Hall is based on the Ashoka Chakra, the depiction of dharmachakra also represented on the national flag. The Central Hall, with its impressive dome just shy of 30 metres in diameter, is a place of exceptional historical significance; it was here, in August 1947, that power was transferred from Britain with the Indian Independence Act.

Sansad Bhavan

New Delhi, India
Edwin Lutyens & Herbert Baker, 1927

Lutyens und Baker, unter deren Ägide bereits die Planung der Kolonialhauptstadt Neu-Delhi erfolgt war, benötigten für den von einer roten Sandsteinmauer gesäumten indischen Parlamentskomplex eine Bauzeit von sechs Jahren. Das Gebäude huldigt indischen Bautraditionen und die kreisrunde Anlage der Central Hall basiert auf dem Ashoka Chakra, der Darstellung des Gesetzesrades oder *Dharmachakra*, das auch die Nationalflagge Indiens ziert. Bei der Central Hall mit ihrer beeindruckenden Kuppel, deren Durchmesser nur knapp unter 30 Meter misst, handelt es sich um einen außerordentlich geschichtsträchtigen Ort, ging hier doch im August 1947 mit dem *Indian Independence Act* die Macht von den Briten auf das unabhängige Indien über.

Le complexe où siège le Parlement indien, encerclé par un mur de grès rouge, a été construit en six ans sous la direction de Lutyens et Baker, alors chargés de concevoir l'aménagement de la capitale coloniale basée à New Delhi. Les bâtiments du parlement rendent hommage aux traditions architecturales de l'Inde, et le plan circulaire de la Salle centrale *(Central Hall)* s'inspire du chakra d'Ashoka, représentation de la roue de Dharma qui figure également sur le drapeau national. La Salle centrale, avec son impressionnante coupole de presque trente mètres de diamètre, est un lieu exceptionnel pour l'histoire d'Inde, puisque c'est entre ses murs, en août 1947, que les Britanniques cédèrent le pouvoir au peuple indien avec la promulgation de la loi proclamant l'indépendance de l'Inde.

El conjunto del Parlamento indio, rodeado por un muro de arenisca rojo, se construyó a lo largo de seis años bajo la dirección de Lutyens y Baker, los responsables de la planificación de la capital colonial de Nueva Delhi. Los edificios del parlamento remiten a las tradiciones arquitectónicas indias: el plano de la Sala Central circular está basado en el chakra de Ashoka, la caracterización de la rueda del dharma que aparece igualmente en la bandera nacional. La Sala Central, con su impresionante cúpula de casi treinta metros de diámetro, reviste un significado histórico excepcional: fue aquí donde, en agosto de 1947, se transfirió el poder de Gran Bretaña a la India gracias al Acta de Independencia de la India.

Jatiyo Sangshad Bhaban

Dhaka, Bangladesh
Louis Kahn, 1982

The Parliament of Bangladesh inhabits one of the world's largest government compounds, covering over 810,000 square metres. Construction began in 1961, but was not completed until 1982, due in great part to the Liberation War and its aftermath. The architect was inspired by the area's aesthetic values and close connection with the landscape, particularly the Ganges Delta. The focal point of the complex is the 30-metre-high assembly chamber, which is surrounded on three sides by an artificial lake. With its exposed concrete walls, geometric apertures and recessed windows, it is at once commanding and connected to the earth on which it stands.

Das Parlament von Bangladesch befindet sich in einer über 809.400 Quadratmeter großen Regierungsanlage, die damit wohl zu den weltweit umfangreichsten ihrer Art zählt. Der Baubeginn erfolgte im Jahr 1961, doch zog sich die Vollendung des Gebäudes vor allem aufgrund der Wirren des Bangladesch-Krieges und seiner Nachwehen bis 1982 hin. Der Architekt inspirierte sich an den ästhetischen Wertvorstellungen und der engen Verbindung zur Landschaft dieser Gegend, insbesondere zum Gangesdelta. Das zentrale Merkmal der Anlage ist der 30 Meter hohe Sitzungssaal, der auf drei Seiten von einem künstlichen See umgeben ist. Die Sichtbetonmauern, geometrischen Öffnungen und zurückgesetzten Fenster verleihen dieser Nationalversammlung ihre gebieterische und gleichzeitig erdverbundene Erscheinung.

Érigé sur plus de 809 400 mètres carrés, le Parlement du Bangladesh figure parmi les bâtiments publics les plus grands du monde. Débutés en 1961, les travaux de construction n'ont été achevés qu'en 1982, principalement en raison de la Guerre de libération et de ses conséquences. L'architecte s'est inspiré des aspects esthétiques du site et de son étroite intégration dans le paysage, notamment le delta du Gange. Point culminant du complexe, l'Assemblée nationale de 30 mètres de haut est bordée sur trois côtés par un lac artificiel. Avec ses murs en béton apparents, ses ouvertures géométriques et ses fenêtres encastrées, le parlement s'impose d'emblée au regard, solidement ancré dans la terre qui l'a vu naître.

El Parlamento de Bangladesh reside
en uno de los mayores recintos
gubernamentales del mundo, con
una extensión que abarca más de 81
hectáreas. Su construcción comenzó
en 1961 pero no finalizó hasta 1982,
debido en gran medida a la Guerra
de Liberación y sus consecuencias.
El arquitecto se inspiró en los valores
estéticos de la zona y en su estrecha
relación con el paisaje, en particular,
el delta del Ganges. El eje central del
conjunto lo constituye la Asamblea
Nacional, con una altura de 30
metros y rodeada en tres de sus
lados por un lago artificial. Gracias
a sus paredes de hormigón visto,
aperturas geométricas y ventanas
empotradas, es a la vez imponente y
cercano a la tierra en la que se yergue.

Ho Chi Minh City, formerly Saigon, is the largest city in Vietnam and the country's administrative hub. The offices of the People's Committee are situated in the former Hôtel de Ville, the French colonial style of which reflects the country's former occupation. Vietnam secured independence in 1945, and Ho Chi Minh, who was instrumental in this fight, is commemorated with a statue in front of the building. The People's Committee is still active within the City Hall, so the public must be satisfied with an external view, which is particularly rewarding at night when illuminated.

Hô-Chi-Minh-Ville, ancienne Saïgon, est la plus grande ville du Vietnam, ainsi que le centre administratif du pays. Les bureaux du Comité populaire se situent dans l'ancien Hôtel de Ville, dont le style colonial français témoigne de l'ancienne occupation du pays. Le Vietnam a accédé à l'indépendance en 1945. Hô Chi Minh, qui a joué un rôle déterminant dans ce combat, y est célébré par une statue à son effigie érigée en face de l'édifice. Le Comité populaire est toujours actif au sein de l'Hôtel de ville, pour le plus grand plaisir du public qui peut profiter de la vue extérieure, particulièrement mise en valeur la nuit une fois illuminée.

La Ciudad de Ho Chi Minh, anteriormente conocida como Saigón, es la mayor ciudad de Vietnam y el centro administrativo del país. Las oficinas del Comité Popular se encuentran en el antiguo Hôtel de Ville, construido en estilo colonial francés, reflejo de la anterior ocupación del país. Vietnam logró la independencia en 1945, lucha en la que Ho Chi Minh desempeñó un papel decisivo, por lo que se le rinde homenaje con una estatua situada frente al edificio. El Comité Popular prosigue sus actividades dentro del ayuntamiento; el público debe conformarse, por lo tanto, con una vista del exterior, especialmente hermosa de noche cuando el edificio está iluminado.

Ho-Chi-Minh-Stadt, das frühere Saigon, ist nicht nur die größte Stadt Vietnams sondern auch das Verwaltungszentrum des Landes. Die Räumlichkeiten des Volkskomitees sind im ehemaligen Hôtel de Ville untergebracht, dessen französischer Kolonialstil die frühere Besatzungsmacht an diesem Ort in Erinnerung ruft. Seine Unabhängigkeit erkämpfte sich Vietnam im Jahr 1945 und vor dem Gebäude wird Ho Chi Minh mit einer Statue gedacht, dem Mann, der dieses Ringen wie kein Zweiter begleitete. Da das Rathaus nach wie vor vom Volkskomitee genutzt wird, bleibt Besuchern nur die Außenansicht des Bauwerks, das dafür jedoch Nacht für Nacht in schönstem Licht erstrahlt.

Ho Chi Minh City Hall

Ho Chi Minh City, Vietnam
1908

New Sarawak State Legislative Assembly (DUN) Building

Kuching, Malaysia
2009

Sarawak is one of two Malaysian states on the island of Borneo. After four centuries of occupation, it was granted independence in 1963, and formed the federation of Malaysia with Malaya, North Borneo and Singapore. The DUN, therefore, situated on the Sarawak River, between the Astana and Fort Margherita, is a symbol of the people's sovereignty and a mark of respect for the state's multi-ethnic population and its achievements in the years since independence. The nine-storey building, with its striking golden roof supported by nine colossal pillars, has quickly been established as an iconic Sarawak landmark.

Sarawak ist einer der beiden malaiischen Bundesstaaten auf der Insel Borneo. Nachdem es vier Jahrhunderte lang besetzt gewesen war, wurde dem Land schließlich 1963 die Unabhängigkeit gewährt, woraufhin es zusammen mit Malaya, Nordborneo und Singapur die Föderation Malaysia ausrief. Aus diesem Grund ist die „Dewan Undangan Negeri" (DUN) oder gesetzgebende Versammlung, die sich am Ufer des Sarawak-Flusses zwischen Astana-Palast und Fort Margherita erhebt, ein Symbol der Herrschaft des Volkes und eine Respektsbezeugung für die multiethnische Bevölkerung des Bundesstaates sowie ihrer Errungenschaften seit der Unabhängigkeit. Das neungeschossige Gebäude mit seinem auffälligen goldenen Dach, das von neun gigantischen Pfeilern getragen wird, wurde im Handumdrehen zu einem Wahrzeichen Sarawaks.

Le Sarawak est l'un des deux états malaysiens situés sur l'île de Bornéo. Après quatre siècles d'occupation, l'état s'est vu accorder l'indépendance en 1963, et forma la fédération de Malaisie avec Malaya, le territoire du Bornéo du Nord et Singapour. Le DUN, alors situé sur la rivière Sarawak, entre l'Astana et Fort Margherita, symbolise la souveraineté du peuple et représente une marque de respect pour la population multiethnique de l'état et pour ses réalisations pendant les années qui suivirent l'indépendance. L'édifice de neuf étages, avec son incroyable toiture dorée posée sur neufs piliers colossaux, s'est rapidement imposé comme un symbole distinctif du Sarawak.

Sarawak constituye uno de los dos estados de Malasia de la isla de Borneo. Después de cuatro siglos de ocupación y tras alcanzar la independencia en 1963, formó la federación de Malasia con Malaya, Borneo Septentrional y Singapur. El DUN, que se encuentra junto al río Sarawak, entre el palacio de Astana y el fuerte Margherita, representa un símbolo de la soberanía popular y un tributo a la población multiétnica del estado y sus logros en los años transcurridos desde la independencia. El edificio de nueve plantas, con su llamativo tejado dorado que se apoya en nueve inmensos pilares, se ha convertido rápidamente en un punto de referencia emblemático de Sarawak.

New Sarawak State Legislative Assembly (DUN) Building, Kuching, Malaysia

Great Hall of the People

Beijing, China
Zhang Bo, 1959

Created as part of the 'Ten Great Constructions' to commemorate the tenth anniversary of the People's Republic of China, this gargantuan edifice was built in just ten months by communist volunteers. The home of the National People's Congress, it is located on the western side of Tiananmen Square, the symbolic birthplace of the PRC. This imposing, Soviet-inspired complex covers a staggering 171,800 square metres, and at its core is the vast Great Auditorium, which can seat 10,000 officials and is topped with a stunning ceiling featuring a red star surrounded by hundreds of lights – representing China's place at the centre of Communism.

Dieser Kolossalbau wurde von kommunistischen Freiwilligen als eines der „Zehn Großen Gebäude" zum zehnjährigen Bestehen der Volksrepublik China in nur zehn Monaten errichtet. Die Heimstatt des Nationalen Volkskongresses erhebt sich an der Westseite des Tian'anmen-Platzes, dem symbolischen Geburtsort der VRC. Diese imposante und stark von Sowjetarchitektur beeinflusste Anlage erstreckt sich über sage und schreibe 171.800 Quadratmeter und beherbergt den Großen Kongresssaal, der bis zu 10.000 Parteifunktionären Platz bietet. Die Decke des Plenarsaals ziert ein von hunderten Lichtern bekränzter roter Stern, der Chinas Platz im Schoß des Kommunismus symbolisiert.

Great Hall of the People, Beijing, China

Construit dans le cadre des
« Dix grands édifices » commandés
pour commémorer le dixième
anniversaire de la République
populaire de Chine, cet ouvrage
gigantesque a été achevé en
seulement dix mois par des bénévoles
communistes. Siège du Congrès
national du Peuple, ce bâtiment
se situe sur l'aile occidentale de la
place Tian'anmen, lieu de naissance
mythique de la RPD. Ce complexe
imposant, inspiré de l'ère soviétique,
s'étend sur une surface stupéfiante
de 171 800 mètres carrés. En son
centre se dresse l'incroyable Grand
auditorium, où peuvent siéger
10 000 représentants, surmonté
d'un remarquable plafond orné
d'une étoile rouge illuminée par des
centaines de lumières, incarnation
de la place centrale qu'occupe
la Chine dans le communisme.

Creado como parte de las «Diez
grandes construcciones» para
conmemorar el décimo aniversario
de la República Popular de China,
este edificio descomunal se levantó
en solo diez meses gracias a la
labor de voluntarios comunistas.
Sede de la Asamblea Popular Nacional,
se encuentra situado al oeste de la
plaza de Tiananmén, cuna simbólica
de la RPC. Esta imponente estructura,
de inspiración soviética, ocupa una
superficie asombrosa de 171.800 metros
cuadrados. En el centro se encuentra
el Gran Auditorio, con cabida para
más de 10.000 personas. Su techo
impresionante muestra una estrella
roja rodeada por centenares de luces:
representa el lugar de China en el
centro del comunismo.

While North Korea is shrouded in secrecy, its use of architecture to project an image of modernity and strength to the rest of the world is well documented. Mansudae Assembly Hall, the home of the Supreme People's Assembly, is no exception. With 50,000 square metres of faced granite and marble, and a main hall with a capacity of 2,000, it certainly makes a statement. The 687 deputies of the Assembly meet here once or twice a year to discuss legislature, although it has been suggested that this is a mere formality – that decisions may have already been made by the nation's executive powers and the Workers' Party, led by Kim Jong-un.

Obwohl Geheimhaltung Nordkoreas oberste Maxime zu sein scheint, lässt sich die Verwendung von Architektur zur globalen Vermittlung der Modernität und Stärke des Landes sehr gut belegen. Die Mansudae-Kongresshalle, der Sitz der Obersten Volksversammlung, ist da keine Ausnahme. Ihre 50.000 Quadratmeter großen und mit Granit und Marmor ausgestatteten Innenflächen sowie ihr Plenarsaal, der bis zu 2000 Personen Platz bietet, setzen ein unmissverständliches Zeichen. Hier treffen sich die 687 Abgeordneten der Nationalversammlung ein bis zwei Mal jährlich, um Fragen der Gesetz-gebung zu erörtern, obwohl bereits darauf hingewiesen wurde, dass es sich dabei lediglich um reine Formalitäten handelt – und sämtliche Entschei-dungen wohl schon im Vorfeld von der Staatsführung sowie der von Kim Jong-un geführten Partei der Arbeit Koreas gefällt werden.

Si la Corée du Nord se drape du plus grand secret, on trouve paradoxalement de nombreux documents sur son utilisation de l'architecture pour projeter l'image d'une nation moderne et forte au reste du monde. La salle de l'Assemblée Mansudae, siège de l'Assemblée suprême du peuple, ne fait pas exception à la règle. Avec sa façade en granit et en marbre de 50 000 mètres carrés et une salle principale d'une capacité de 2 000 sièges, l'édifice en impose clairement. Les 687 députés de l'Assemblée se réunissent ici une fois voire deux fois par an pour y débattre de la législation, même si, selon certains, il s'agirait en réalité d'une simple formalité, les décisions ayant déjà été prises par le pouvoir exécutif de la nation et par le Parti du travail dirigé par Kim Jong-un.

Aunque Corea del Norte está envuelta en un manto de secretismo, el uso que hace de la arquitectura para proyectar una imagen de modernidad y fuerza al resto el mundo está más que demostrado. El Palacio de Congresos de Mansudae, la sede de la Asamblea Suprema del Pueblo, no constituye ninguna excepción a esto. Con una fachada de 50.000 metros cuadrados de granito y mármol y un salón de actos principal capaz de acoger a 2.000 personas, no cabe duda de que es toda una declaración de intenciones. Los 687 diputados de la asamblea se reúnen aquí una o dos veces al año para debatir sobre leyes, aunque se comenta que se trata de una pura formalidad: el poder ejecutivo de la nación y el Partido de los Trabajadores, dirigidos por Kim Jong-un, se han encargado ya de tomar las decisiones.

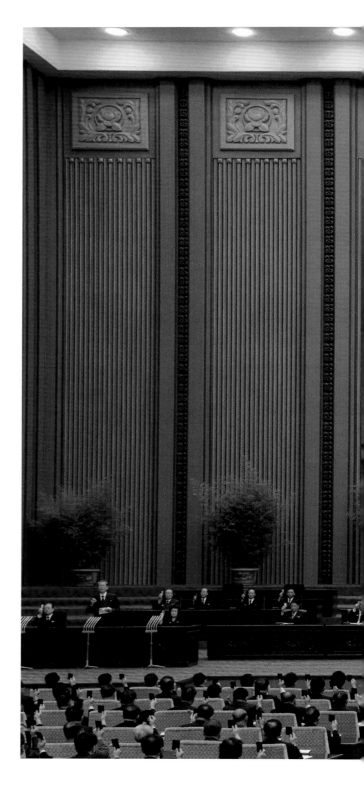

Mansudae Assembly Hall

Pyongyang, Democratic People's Republic of Korea
1984

National Assembly Building

Seoul, South Korea
1975

Located on Yeouido Island,
the National Assembly Building of
South Korea is a stately but somewhat
defensive structure. It is surrounded
by twenty-four unembellished granite
pillars, symbolising the twenty-four
solar terms of the Korean calendar,
and a striking green dome crowns eight
storeys – six above ground, two below.
While the Assembly has 300 members
at present, the main chamber has been
built to accommodate 400, should
Korean reunification be realised,
but there remains a pervading sense
of watchfulness; the complex is heavily
guarded, protecting not only this
grand building, but the hard-fought
democracy to which South Koreans
are so committed.

Bei der auf der Insel Yeouido gelegenen
und in der Landessprache *Gukhoe*
genannten Nationalversammlung
Südkoreas handelt es sich um eine
sowohl herrschaftlich als auch
bisweilen defensiv anmutende Anlage.
Vierundzwanzig schmucklose Granit-
pfeiler, welche die 24 Solarperioden
des koreanischen Kalenders
symbolisieren, umringen den Bau,
dessen sechs oberirdische und
zwei unterirdische Geschosse von
einer augenfälligen grünen Kuppel
bekrönt werden. Die im Hinblick auf
eine mögliche Wiedervereinigung
Koreas für 400 Abgeordnete
konzipierte Gukhoe dient heute
300 Parlamentariern als Wirkstätte,
wiewohl sich der Eindruck einer alles
durchdringenden Wachsamkeit nicht
leugnen lässt; die strenge Bewachung
der Anlage dient nicht nur dem
Gebäude selbst, sondern auch und
gerade der hart erkämpften Demokratie,
der sich Südkorea verschrieben hat.

Situé sur l'île de Yeouido, le bâtiment
où siège l'Assemblée nationale de Corée
du Sud arbore une structure certes
gouvernementale mais aux allures
défensives. L'édifice est entouré de
vingt-quatre piliers de granit sobres,
symbolisant les vingt-quatre tournants
solaires du calendrier coréen, et un
surprenant dôme vert vient surmonter
huit étages, dont six s'élèvent au-dessus
du sol, et deux sous terre. Si l'assemblée
compte 300 membres à l'heure actuelle,
la salle principale a été construite
pour accueillir 400 personnes,
dans l'hypothèse où la réunification
de la Corée aurait lieu. L'édifice est
cependant empreint d'un sentiment
diffus de vigilance ; le complexe fait en
effet l'objet d'une étroite surveillance.
Cette protection vise bien sûr l'immense
bâtiment mais aussi la démocratie
acquise de haute lutte à laquelle
les Sud-coréens sont si attachés.

Situado en la isla de Yeouido, el edificio de la Asamblea Nacional de Corea del Sur muestra una estructura majestuosa pero con un carácter un tanto defensivo. Está rodeado por veinticuatro columnas de granito, sin adornos, que simbolizan los veinticuatro períodos solares del calendario coreano. Una llamativa cúpula verde corona las ocho plantas: seis en la superficie y dos bajo tierra. Aunque la asamblea está formada actualmente por 300 miembros, la cámara principal se construyó para acoger a 400, en previsión de la reunificación de Corea. Permanece, no obstante, cierta idea dominante de cautela: el conjunto está fuertemente vigilado para proteger no solo el edificio sino la democracia ganada a pulso, a la que tan entregados están los surcoreanos.

Also known as Tokyo City Hall, this domineering structure is home to the Tokyo Metropolitan Government. Located in Shinjuku, it comprises three buildings, each occupying a city block; the tallest of these stands at a towering forty-eight storeys, and splits in two on the thirty-third floor, which offers a futuristic take on the Gothic cathedral. The architect's concept was inspired by a computer chip, and although the external textured finish is inspired by traditional Japanese architecture, the overall design is decidedly European, reflecting the post-modern propensities of 1980s architecture.

Tokyo Metropolitan Government Building

Tokyo, Japan
Kenzō Tange, 1990

Dieser imposante und auch als Tokyo City Hall bekannte Gebäudekomplex ist der Verwaltungssitz der Präfektur Tokio. Er liegt in Shinjuku und umfasst drei Bauten, die jeder für sich einen Häuserblock einnehmen; der höchste der drei Türme ragt auf gewaltige 84 Stockwerke auf und gabelt sich im 33. Geschoss, was der gothischen Kathedrale ein futuristisches Etwas verleiht. Der Entwurf lehnt sich an einen Computerchip an und obwohl die äußere Oberflächenausführung von traditioneller japanischer Architektur inspiriert ist, folgt die Gesamtausführung dezidiert europäischen Konzepten und spiegelt postmoderne Architekturvorlieben der 1980er-Jahre.

Également appelée Hôtel de ville de Tokyo, cette structure colossale accueille le Gouvernement métropolitain de Tokyo. Situé dans le quartier de Shinjuku, le complexe se compose de trois bâtiments qui occupent chacun un bloc entier de la ville ; le plus haut d'entre eux domine le paysage du haut de ses quarante-huit étages, puis se divise en deux au niveau du trente-troisième étage pour recréer la forme futuriste d'une cathédrale gothique. L'architecte dit s'être inspiré d'une puce électronique. Bien que la finition extérieure rappelle par sa texture l'architecture japonaise traditionnelle, le style général de la structure est résolument européen, à l'image du courant architectural post-moderne des années 80.

Esta estructura dominante, conocida también como el Ayuntamiento de Tokio, es la sede del Gobierno Metropolitano de Tokio. Situada en Shinjuku, consta de tres edificios, cada uno de los cuales ocupa una manzana. El más alto de ellos, una torre de cuarenta y ocho plantas que se divide en dos en el piso treinta y tres, recrea la apariencia futurista de una catedral gótica. El arquitecto se inspiró, para su concepto, en un chip de ordenador y, aunque el acabado con relieve exterior está basado en la arquitectura japonesa tradicional, en líneas generales, el diseño es indudablemente europeo. Refleja las exuberancias posmodernas de la arquitectura de la década de 1980.

Tokyo Metropolitan Government Building, Tokyo, Japan

Parliament House

Canberra, Australia
Romaldo Giurgola, 1988

In 1901, the Australian colonies united to form the Commonwealth of Australia, and in 1909 Canberra was chosen as the site for the new capital. A temporary building was erected in 1927, and in 1978 plans were announced to construct a permanent parliament. This new complex, built entirely from materials sourced in Australia, is one of the largest buildings in the southern hemisphere and attracts approximately 1 million visitors per year. Postmodern in style, the deceptively simple structure is enhanced by clever landscaping, nods to national history, art and culture, and of course the iconic steel flagpole, which towers at 81 metres tall, a landmark for the city of Canberra.

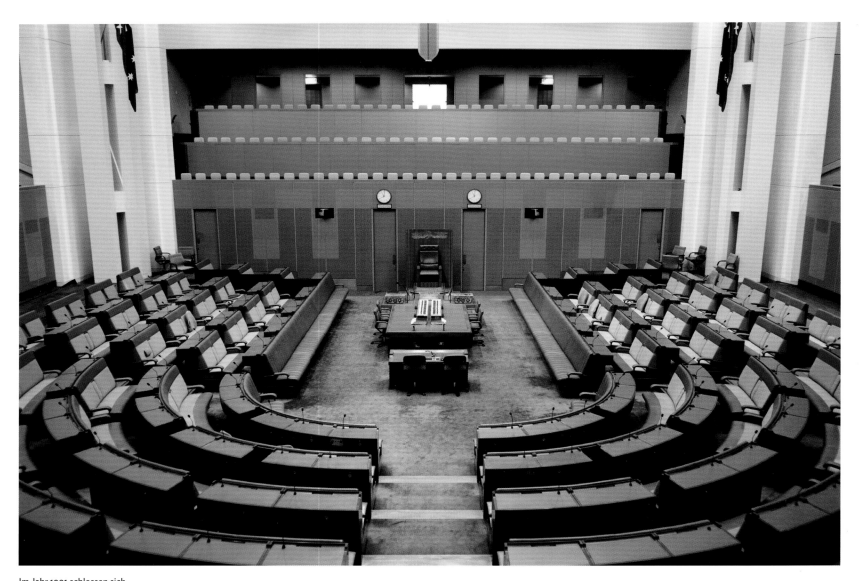

Im Jahr 1901 schlossen sich
sämtliche Kolonien Australiens
zum Commonwealth of Australia
zusammen und Canberra wurde 1909
zum Standort der neuen Hauptstadt
bestimmt. Ein Übergangsgebäude
wurde im Jahr 1927 errichtet und 1978
folgte die Bekanntgabe der Errichtung
eines dauerhaften Parlaments.
Dieser neue und vollständig aus in
Australien verfügbaren Werkstoffen
errichtete Komplex ist eines der
größten Bauwerke der südlichen
Hemisphäre und lockt jährlich bis
zu einer Million Besucher an diesen
Ort. Die postmoderne und trügerisch
einfache Struktur wird durch eine
geschickte Landschaftgestaltung
sowie Verweise auf die Geschichte,
Kunst und Kultur des Landes ergänzt
und natürlich durch den unver-
kennbaren stählernen Flaggenmast,
der mit seinen 81 Metern Höhe zu den
Wahrzeichen der Stadt Canberra zählt.

Parliament House, Canberra, Australia

En 1901, les colonies australiennes se sont réunies pour former le Commonwealth d'Australie. En 1909, Canberra fut choisie comme nouvelle capitale. Un bâtiment provisoire fut érigé en 1927, et le projet de construction d'un parlement permanent fut annoncé en 1978. Ce nouveau complexe, entièrement construit avec des matériaux d'origine australienne, est l'un des bâtiments les plus vastes de l'hémisphère Sud et accueille près d'un million de visiteurs par an. De style post-moderne, la structure à l'allure faussement sobre est mise en valeur par de judicieux aménagements paysagers, par d'habiles références à l'histoire nationale, à l'art et à la culture, et bien sûr par le mât en acier emblématique qui culmine à 81 mètres de haut, véritable jalon pour la ville de Canberra.

En 1901, las colonias de Australia se unieron para formar la Commonwealth de Australia y, en 1909, se eligió Canberra como sede de la nueva capital. Tras la construcción en 1927 de un edificio provisional, no fue hasta 1978 cuando se anunció un plan para construir un parlamento permanente. Este nuevo complejo, creado en su totalidad a partir de materiales originarios de Australia, es uno de los edificios más grandes del hemisferio sur y atrae aproximadamente a un millón de visitantes al año. De estilo posmoderno, la estructura aparentemente sencilla destaca gracias a un inteligente paisajismo, a las alusiones a la historia, el arte y la cultura nacionales y, por supuesto, al emblemático mástil de acero que alcanza los 81 metros de altura, un punto de referencia para la ciudad de Canberra.

Parliament Buildings

Wellington, New Zealand
John Campbell, 1922
Basil Spence, 1977

When its predecessor was destroyed by fire in 1907, a competition was launched to design a new building for the New Zealand Parliament. Designs by John Campbell came first and fourth, so the two were combined, and construction on the first phase began in 1914. Progress was slow, however, because of the First World War. It was finished in 1922, but the second phase was abandoned. The executive wing, 'The Beehive', was conceived by Basil Spence and opened in 1977. At 72 metres high, and crowned with a distinctive copper roof, it stands in sharp contrast to its older, neoclassical sibling, with its imposing columns of indigenous Takaka marble.

Als das Vorgängergebäude 1907 einem Feuer zum Opfer fiel, wurde ein Wettbewerb ausgeschrieben, um den Entwurf für das neue Parlament Neuseelands zu ermitteln. Da John Campbell mit zweien seiner Entwürfe den ersten und den vierten Platz errang, wurden beide miteinander kombiniert; die erste Bauphase wurde im Jahr 1914 in Angriff genommen. Aufgrund der Wirren des ersten Weltkriegs kam die Errichtung jedoch nur schleppend voran; zwar kam es 1922 zur Vollendung des ersten Abschnitts, doch wurde auf die zweite Bauphase vollständig verzichtet. Der auch als „The Beehive" (zu Deutsch: „Der Bienenstock") bezeichnete Flügel der Exekutive wurde von Basil Spence entworfen und 1977 eingeweiht. Mit einer Höhe von 72 Metern und seinem unverwechselbaren Kupferdach hebt sich dieser Bau deutlich von den älteren neoklassizistischen Nebengebäuden mit ihren imposanten Säulen aus einheimischem Takaka-Marmor ab.

Après un incendie destructeur en 1907, un concours fut lancé pour construire le nouveau Parlement néozélandais. Les maquettes de John Campbell arrivèrent première et quatrième du concours. Elles furent donc fusionnées, et la première phase des travaux de construction débuta en 1914. Ralentie par la Première Guerre mondiale, cette première phase ne fut toutefois achevée qu'en 1922, alors que la seconde phase fut abandonnée. L'aile administrative baptisée « The Beehive » (la Ruche) a été édifiée par Basil Spence et ouverte en 1977. Du haut de ses 72 mètres, surmontée d'un toit en cuivre, la Ruche contraste avec son ancien prédécesseur de style néoclassique, et ses deux colonnes imposantes en marbre local de Takaka.

Cuando en 1907 un incendio destruyó el edificio anterior, se organizó un concurso con el fin de diseñar una nueva estructura para el Parlamento neozelandés. Los diseños de John Campbell quedaron en primer y en cuarto lugar, por lo que tras combinarlos, en 1914, comenzó la construcción de la primera fase. A pesar del lento avance, debido a la Primera Guerra Mundial, el edificio se terminó en 1922, aunque se abandonó la idea de una segunda fase. El ala administrativa «La Colmena», obra de Basil Spence, se inauguró en 1977. Con 72 metros de altura y rematado por su característico tejado cobrizo, contrasta marcadamente con su antecesor neoclásico, gracias a sus imponentes columnas de mármol de Takaka autóctono.

Los Angeles City Hall

Los Angeles, USA
John B. Parkinson, John C. Austin, Albert C. Martin Sr, 1928

City Hall is perhaps the most famous building in Los Angeles; it features on all official city documents, on police badges, and is a frequent supporting player in film, television and gaming. Austin classed the building as 'Modern American'; although influenced by a great many styles, the aim was to create a heretofore unseen mode of architecture. The 138-metre tower, however, is unmistakably art deco in style. No building in Los Angeles was allowed to exceed its height for many years, and it remained the tallest building in the state until 1964. In 2001, a seismic retrofit was completed to protect City Hall from serious damage from earthquakes, to which the city is prone.

Bei der City Hall handelt es sich um das wohl berühmteste Gebäude der Stadt Los Angeles; es findet sich auf sämtlichen offiziellen Dokumenten der Stadt, auf den Polizeiabzeichen und spielt in zahlreichen Filmen, Fernsehsendungen und Videospielen eine bedeutende Nebenrolle. Austin klassifizierte den Stil seines Gebäudes als „Modern American"; obwohl etliche Baustile Pate standen, sollte mit diesem Gebäude doch eine bisher noch nie dagewesene Architekturform geschaffen werden, auch wenn der 138 Meter hohe Turm unverkennbar im Art-déco-Stil gehalten ist. Lange Zeit durfte kein anderes Gebäude der Stadt die City Hall überragen und tatsächlich war das Rathaus von Los Angeles bis 1964 das höchste Bauwerk in ganz Kalifornien. Im Jahr 2001 wurde es einer seismischen Nachrüstung unterzogen, um den Sitz der Stadtverwaltung vor ernstzunehmenden Schäden durch Erdbeben zu bewahren, welche die Stadt der Engel seit jeher bedrohen.

Los Angeles City Hall, Los Angeles, USA

City Hall (Hôtel de ville) est sans doute l'édifice le plus connu de Los Angeles ; il figure dans tous les documents officiels de la ville, sur les badges de la police, et sert fréquemment de décor pour le cinéma, la télévision et les jeux. Austin a vu dans cet ouvrage « le style américain moderne » ; malgré d'innombrables influences architecturales, l'objectif était de créer un style jusqu'alors jamais vu. Pour autant, la tour de 138 mètres de haut est résolument d'inspiration Art déco. Il a longtemps été interdit de construire des immeubles dépassant le City Hall qui demeura l'édifice le plus haut de l'état jusqu'en 1964. En 2001, le City Hall fit l'objet de modernisations antisismiques afin de prévenir les risques importants de tremblements de terre auxquels la ville est soumise.

El Ayuntamiento, City Hall, es quizá el edificio más famoso de los Ángeles, ya que aparece en todos los documentos oficiales de la ciudad, en las placas de la policía y, como actor secundario habitual, en el cine, la televisión y los juegos de azar. Austin clasificó el edificio como «Modern American»: aunque influido por una gran variedad de estilos, el objetivo era crear una modalidad de arquitectura nunca vista hasta la fecha. La torre de 138 metros, no obstante, presenta un estilo inconfundiblemente Art deco. Durante años, ningún edificio de Los Ángeles tuvo el permiso de superar su altura, por lo que siguió siendo el edificio más alto del estado hasta 1964. En 2001, concluyó la modernización sísmica para proteger el Ayuntamiento de posibles graves daños provocados por los terremotos, a los que la ciudad es propensa.

National Palace

Mexico City, Mexico
16th Century – 1929

The National Palace is home to the Federal Executive of Mexico, but this site has been the seat of leadership since Aztec times. Initially this was the location of the palaces of Moctezuma II, but from the 1500s Spanish viceroys adapted the complex to their tastes. With the dawn of independence, further changes were made, including the addition of the third floor. The architecture, as a result, is a blend of Aztec and Spanish elements; a perfect representation of the people. Highlights include the frescoes by Diego Rivera, depicting the history of the nation, and the Freedom Bell, which is rung every 15 September to mark the start of the War of Independence.

Der Palacio Nacional ist der Sitz der mexikanischen Regierung, doch dient sein Standort bereits seit der Zeit der Azteken der Ausübung von Macht. Ursprünglich befand sich hier die Palastanlage Moctezumas II., bevor im 15. Jahrhundert die Vizekönige Spaniens den Komplex in ihrem Sinne umzugestalten begannen. Am Vorabend der Unabhängigkeit wurden weitere Veränderungen durchgeführt, darunter die Erweiterung auf drei Stockwerke. Aufgrund seiner Geschichte ist die Architektur des Nationalpalastes eine Mischung aus aztekischen und spanischen Elementen – und allein dadurch eine würdige Vertretung des mexikanischen Volkes. Zu den Glanzstücken zählen die Fresken Diego Riveras, welche die Landesgeschichte schildern, sowie die Freiheitsglocke, die alljährlich am 15. September geläutet wird, um an den Beginn des Unabhängigkeitskrieges zu gemahnen.

Le Palais national est le siège du pouvoir exécutif fédéral au Mexique. Ce site a toutefois été un centre du pouvoir depuis l'époque aztèque. Il hébergeait à l'origine les palais de Moctezuma II, mais à partir des années 1500, les vice-rois espagnols adaptèrent le complexe au gré de leurs convenances. À l'aube de l'indépendance, de nouvelles transformations eurent lieu, dont l'ajout d'un troisième niveau. Le palais arbore ainsi un style architectural hétéroclite mélangeant éléments aztèques et espagnols, dans une parfaite représentation du peuple. Le monument compte au nombre de ses attractions les fresques de Diego Rivera qui retracent l'histoire de la nation, et la Cloche de la liberté qui retentit chaque 15 septembre pour célébrer le début de la Guerre d'indépendance.

En el Palacio Nacional se halla la sede del poder ejecutivo federal de México pero este lugar ha sido centro de poder desde época azteca. Aquí se encontraba el emplazamiento inicial de los palacios de Moctezuma II, aunque desde el siglo XVI los virreyes españoles adaptaron el edificio a su gusto. En los albores de la independencia, se realizaron más modificaciones, entre ellas, la construcción de la tercera planta. La arquitectura es, por lo tanto, una combinación de elementos aztecas y españoles: una perfecta representación del pueblo. Entre los elementos más destacados se incluyen los frescos de Diego Rivera, que describen la historia de la nación, y la Campana de la Libertad, cuyo tañido resuena cada 15 de septiembre en conmemoración del inicio de la Guerra de la Independencia.

National Palace, Mexico City, Mexico

National Capitol Building

Havana, Cuba
Raúl Otero & Eugenio Rayneri Piedra, 1929

‚El Capitolio' wurde vom kubanischen Präsidenten Gerardo Machado nach seiner Wahl 1925 in Auftrag gegeben und diente bis zum Ende der Kubanischen Revolution und der Machtübernahme durch die Kommunisten im Jahr 1959 als Regierungssitz. Eine Zeit lang beherbergte es das Ministerium für Wissenschaft, Technologie und Umwelt, doch kündigte die Regierung 2013 an, sie gedenke, dem Kapitol seinen einstigen Glanz wiederzugeben und den Sitz der Nationalversammlung dorthin zu verlegen. Das auf fünf Jahre ausgelegte Restaurierungsvorhaben soll diesen einstigen Ausbund an Extravaganz in Kubas kommunistisches Parlament verwandeln.

'El Capitolio' was commissioned by President Gerardo Machado after his 1925 election, and it was the seat of government until the Cuban Revolution ended in 1959, when the Communist regime was established. For a time it housed the Ministry of Science, Technology and the Environment, but in 2013 the government announced its plans to restore the Capitol to its former glory and make it home to the National Assembly. The restoration project, which is expected to take around five years, will see this former paragon of extravagance become home to Cuba's Communist parliament.

National Capitol Building, Havana, Cuba

Commandé par le Président Gerardo
Machado après avoir été élu en
1925, « El Capitolio » a été le siège
du gouvernement jusqu'à la fin
de la Révolution cubaine en 1959,
année de la mise en place du régime
communiste. Le bâtiment a un temps
hébergé le ministère des Sciences,
de la Technologie et de l'Environnement.
Toutefois, en 2013, le gouvernement
a annoncé le projet de restaurer le
Capitole dans sa splendeur d'antan
pour en faire le siège de l'Assemblée
nationale. Les travaux de restauration,
qui devraient durer cinq ans
environ, feront de cet ancien modèle
d'extravagance le nouveau siège
du parlement communiste de Cuba.

El Capitolio, realizado por encargo
del presidente Gerardo Machado
tras su elección en 1925, fue la sede del
gobierno hasta el final de la Revolución
Cubana en 1959, cuando se estableció
el régimen comunista. Durante un
tiempo, albergó el Ministerio de
Ciencias, Tecnología y Medio Ambiente,
pero en 2013 el gobierno anunció
un plan para devolver al Capitolio
su antiguo esplendor y convertirlo
en la sede de la asamblea nacional.
El proyecto de restauración, que se
prevé que dure unos cinco años,
convertirá este antiguo ejemplo de
derroche en la sede del parlamento
comunista de Cuba.

Toronto City Hall

Toronto, Canada
*Viljo Revell, with Heikki Castren,
Bengt Lundsten & Seppo Valius, 1965*

In 1958 an international competition
to design Toronto's New City Hall
was launched by Mayor Nathan Phillips
(for whom the square in front of the
edifice is now named). The winning
design could not have been further
removed from that of its adjacent
Romanesque Revival predecessor,
which is now a courthouse. In Revell's
modern design a podium supports
a council chamber embraced by two
towers of differing heights; the east
tower stands at twenty-seven storeys,
and the west tower at twenty. The curve
of these towers and the white disk of
the chamber, when viewed from the air,
led to the complex's playful nickname:
'The Eye of the Government'.

Im Jahr 1958 suchten die Stadtoberen
rund um Bürgermeister Nathan Phillips
(nach dem der Vorplatz des Gebäudes
schließlich benannt wurde) mithilfe
einer internationalen Ausschreibung
den Entwurf für Torontos neue City
Hall. Das Siegerdesign hätte sich kaum
mehr von seinem benachbarten und
heute als Gerichtsgebäude dienenden
Vorgänger in neoromanischem Stil
unterscheiden können. Mithilfe eines
Podiums stützt Revells moderner
Entwurf den Ratssaal, der wiederum
von zwei Türmen unterschiedlicher
Höhe flankiert wird; der Ostturm
verfügt über 27 Stockwerke,
während der Westturm 20 Geschosse
aufweist. Aus der Vogelperspektive
wird deutlich, wie die Wölbung
der Türme und die weiße Scheibe
des Plenarsaals der Anlage zu
ihrem nicht ganz ernst gemeinten
Spitznamen „Eye of the Government"
oder „Regierungsauge" verhalfen.

En 1958, le maire Nathan Phillips (dont le nom a été donné à la place située devant l'édifice) lance un concours d'architecture international pour concevoir le futur Hôtel de ville de Toronto. On ne pouvait imaginer projet gagnant plus dissemblable que son prédécesseur attenant de style néo-roman, qui abrite désormais le palais de justice. L'architecture moderne de Revell repose sur une estrade qui accueille une salle du conseil flanquée de deux tours de hauteur différente ; la tour orientale s'élève sur vingt-sept étages, contre vingt pour la tour occidentale. La cambrure de ces deux tours et le disque blanc formé par la salle du conseil, vus d'en haut, ont valu au complexe le surnom « d'œil du gouvernement ».

En 1958, el alcalde Nathan Phillips (que dio nombre a la actual plaza frente al edificio) organizó un concurso internacional para diseñar el nuevo ayuntamiento de Toronto. El diseño ganador no pudo distanciarse más del de su predecesor adyacente de estilo neorrománico, ocupado actualmente por un juzgado. En el moderno diseño de Revell, un podio soporta un salón de plenos rodeado por dos torres de distintas alturas: la torre este presenta veintisiete plantas y la oeste, veinte. La curva de estas torres y el disco blanco del salón de plenos, cuando se aprecian desde el aire, han generado un malicioso apodo para el conjunto: «El Ojo del Gobierno».

The cast-iron dome of the Capitol, the seat of the United States Congress, is arguably the most recognisable man-made landmark in the USA. At its pinnacle, giving the Capitol a total height of 88 metres, stands the 'Statue of Freedom', which, together with the overall neoclassical approach, reflects the ancient ideals of governance for the people, by the people. This design was selected by President George Washington, who laid the cornerstone in 1793, but construction was slow, owing to funding difficulties and the War of 1812, and over time involved eleven different architects. Today, the Capitol covers approximately 16,200 square metres and is one of the world's most popular federal buildings, with 3-5 million global visitors annually.

Die gusseiserne Kuppel des Kapitols, des Sitzes des US-Kongresses, stellt wohl unzweifelhaft das charakteristischste menschengemachte Wahrzeichen in den gesamten Vereinigten Staaten dar. Die über der Kuppelspitze aufragende Statue der Freiheit verleiht dem Kapitol eine Gesamthöhe von 88 Metern und bezeugt, wie auch der neoklassizistische Gesamtstil des Gebäudes, die einstigen Ideale einer Regierung für das Volk durch das Volk. Ausgewählt wurde der Entwurf von Präsident George Washington, der 1793 höchstselbst den Grundstein legte. Allein, aufgrund finanzieller Probleme sowie des Krieges von 1812 beschäftigte der Bau insgesamt elf Architekten und ging nur sehr schleppend voran. Das heutige Kapitol erstreckt sich über gut 16.000 Quadratmeter und zählt zu den berühmtesten bundesstaatlichen Gebäuden der Welt, wovon nicht zuletzt die 3-5 Millionen Besucher pro Jahr Zeugnis ablegen.

United States Capitol

Washington, D.C., USA
William Thornton, 1800

Le dôme en fonte du Capitole, siège du Congrès américain, est incontestablement l'ouvrage architectural le plus distinctif des États-Unis. En son sommet, faisant culminer le Capitole à 88 mètres de haut, se dresse la Statue de la Liberté qui, avec le style général de l'édifice d'inspiration néoclassique, incarne les antiques idéaux de gouvernance du peuple par le peuple. Le projet a été choisi par le Président George Washington, qui posa la première pierre de l'édifice en 1793. Les travaux de construction ont été cependant ralentis par des problèmes de financement et par la Guerre anglo-américaine de 1812. La construction du Capitole a vu se succéder onze architectes en tout. Aujourd'hui, le Capitole s'étend sur près de 16 000 mètres carrés et représente l'un des édifices fédéraux les plus connus au monde qui accueille 3 à 5 millions de visiteurs par an.

La cúpula de hierro fundido del Capitolio, sede del Congreso de los Estados Unidos, es posiblemente el emblema arquitectónico más reconocible de este país. En su pináculo, que proporciona al Capitolio una altura total de 88 metros, se encuentra la Estatua de la Libertad que, junto con el planteamiento neoclásico del conjunto, encarna los antiguos ideales de gobierno para el pueblo y por el pueblo. El diseño fue seleccionado por el presidente George Washington, que colocó la piedra angular en 1793, pero la construcción se llevó a cabo lentamente, debido a problemas financieros y a la Guerra de 1812, y a lo largo del tiempo requirió la participación de once arquitectos distintos. Actualmente, el Capitolio abarca aproximadamente una hectárea y media y es uno de los edificios federales más conocidos del mundo, con un total de entre 3 y 5 millones de visitantes anuales.

Parliament Buildings

Ottawa, Canada
Thomas Fuller & Chilion Jones, Thomas Stent & Augustus Laver, 1866
John A. Pearson & Jean Omer Marchand, 1922

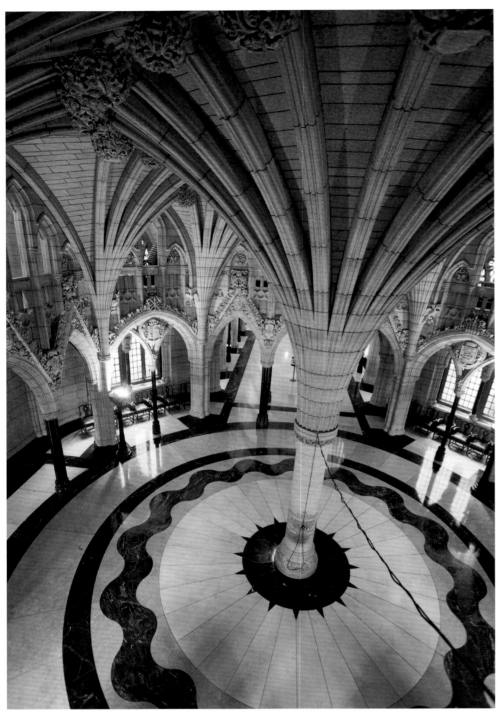

Im Jahr 1857 wurde Ottawa von Königin Victoria zur Hauptstadt der Provinz Kanada bestimmt und nur zwei Jahre später erfolgte an einer den Fluss Ottawa überragenden Stelle der erste Spatenstich zu diesem Gebäude. Der zentrale sowie der Ost- und West-Block wurden 1866 fertiggestellt und im darauffolgenden Jahr stieg Kanada im Rahmen des British North America Act zu einem selbstverwaltenden Dominion auf. Der ursprüngliche zentrale Block fiel 1916 einem Brand zum Opfer, doch ging man noch vor Ende des ersten Weltkrieges an die Wiedererrichtung. Vollendet wurde das zu Ehren Westminsters im neo-gotischen Stil erbaute und bewusst als Gegenentwurf zum neoklassizistischen US-Kapitol gehaltene neue Gebäude schließlich 1922.

In 1857, Queen Victoria chose Ottawa as the capital of the Province of Canada, and work began soon after, in 1859, on a site overlooking the Ottawa River. The Centre, East and West blocks were completed by 1866, and the following year Canada became a country under the terms of the British North America Act. The original Centre Block was devastated by fire in 1916, and rebuilding commenced during the First World War. The new building was completed in 1922, its Gothic Revival style chosen both in homage to Westminster and in deliberate contrast to the neoclassical US Capitol.

Parliament Buildings, Ottawa, Canada

Parliament Buildings, Ottawa, Canada

En 1857, la Reine Victoria désigna Ottawa capitale de la Province du Canada. Des travaux de construction débutèrent peu après, en 1859, sur un site surplombant la rivière des Outaouais. Les parties Centrale, Orientale et Occidentale furent achevées en 1866, et l'année suivante, le Canada fut proclamé pays aux termes de l'Acte de l'Amérique du Nord britannique. L'édifice central d'origine fut dévasté par un incendie en 1916, puis reconstruit durant la Première Guerre mondiale. Le nouvel édifice fut achevé en 1922, dans un style néo-gothique choisi à la fois pour rendre hommage à Westminster et prendre délibérément le contrepied du Capitole américain et de son style néoclassique.

En 1857, la reina Victoria eligió Ottawa como capital de la Provincia de Canadá, tras lo que se iniciaron las obras, en 1859, en un emplazamiento sobre el río Ottawa. Los bloques Centro, Este y Oeste se terminaron en 1866 y, un año después, Canadá se convirtió en un país soberano según lo previsto en el Acta de la Norteamérica británica. El bloque Centro original fue destruido por un incendio en 1916 y su reconstrucción comenzó durante la Primera Guerra Mundial. El nuevo edificio, finalizado en 1922, es de carácter neogótico, estilo que se eligió tanto en homenaje a Westminster como en marcado contraste con el neoclasicismo del Capitolio de EE. UU.

La Casa Rosada

Buenos Aires, Argentina
1886

This enigmatic building, which houses the office of the president and the government of Argentina, is perhaps best known internationally for the iconic speeches delivered from its balconies by Eva Perón and General Leopoldo Galtieri. The mansion has been declared a National Historic Monument, and its distinctive external hue is a subject of debate. Some say this combination of the red of the Federalists and the white of the Unitarians was a gesture to ease political tensions in the 1870s; others that it is simply the result of being painted with cow blood, a once common practice to protect against humidity.

Dieses schillernde Gebäude beherbergt das Büro des Staatspräsidenten sowie die Regierung des Landes und ist im Ausland wohl vor allem aufgrund der einzigartigen Ansprachen bekannt, die etwa von Eva Perón oder von General Leopoldo Galtieri auf einem seiner Balkone gehalten wurden. Das Anwesen wurde zum Nationalen Historischen Monument erklärt und seine unverwechselbare Fassade ist Gegenstand vieler Diskussionen. Einige behaupten, dass die Kombination aus dem Rot der Föderalisten und dem Weiß der Unitarier der Besänftigung der politischen Spannungen der 1870er-Jahre dienen sollte; andere wiederum, dass sich der Farbton ganz einfach aus dem Anstrich mit Rinderblut erkläre, einer einst weitverbreiteten Praxis zum Schutz gegen Feuchtigkeit.

Cet édifice énigmatique, qui abrite le bureau du Président, ainsi que le Gouvernement d'Argentine, est sans doute mieux connu dans le monde pour les célèbres discours prononcés depuis ses balcons par Eva Perón et le Général Leopoldo Galtieri. L'édifice a été proclamé monument historique national, et sa couleur extérieure distinctive ne cesse d'alimenter les débats. Certains affirment que cette association entre le rouge des Fédéralistes et le blanc des Unitaires symbolise un geste visant à apaiser les tensions politiques dans les années 1870 ; d'autres que cette couleur résulte tout simplement d'une peinture au sang de bœuf, pratique alors courante pour protéger les bâtiments contre l'humidité.

Este enigmático edificio, que alberga las oficinas del presidente y del Gobierno de Argentina, es quizá más conocido, a nivel internacional, por los emblemáticos discursos pronunciados desde sus balcones por Eva Perón y el general Leopoldo Galtieri. La mansión ha sido declarada Monumento Histórico Nacional y su característico tono exterior es objeto de debate. Unos cuentan que esta combinación del rojo de los federales y del blanco de los unitarios fue un gesto para aliviar las tensiones políticas en la década de 1870; otros, que es simplemente el resultado de pintarlo con sangre de vaca, una práctica común en su día para proteger las casas contra la humedad.

First proposed in the eighteenth century in an effort to spread national resources and divert the concentration of investment away from Rio de Janeiro, the planned capital of Brasília was realised by President Juscelino Kubitschek in the 1950s. He initiated a flurry of construction, as innovative buildings were erected to reflect an open and progressive new capital, under the direction of Oscar Niemeyer and Lúcio Costa. The Congresso Nacional, which is comprised of two twenty-eight-storey towers flanked by the dome-shaped senate and the bowl-shaped Chamber of Deputies, is the jewel in the crown of this UNESCO World Heritage site.

Zwar wurde die Gründung einer neuen brasilianischen Hauptstadt bereits im 18. Jahrhundert ins Auge gefasst, um die Nutzung nationaler Ressourcen zu streuen und Investitionen außerhalb Rio de Janeiros anzukurbeln, doch konnte das am Reißbrett geplante Brasília schlussendlich erst in den 1950er-Jahren von Präsident Juscelino Kubitschek aus der Taufe gehoben werden. Er gab den Startschuss für eine rege Bautätigkeit, deren Ziel es war, mithilfe innovativer Gebäude und unter der Leitung von Oscar Niemeyer und Lúcio Costa die Offenheit und Progressivität der neuen Kapitale widerzuspiegeln. Der aus zwei 28-geschossigen Türmen, dem angrenzenden kuppelförmigen Senat sowie der schalenförmigen Abgeordnetenkammer bestehende Congresso Nacional ist das unangefochtene Kleinod dieser UNESCO-Weltkulturerbestätte.

National Congress Building

Brasília, Brazil
Oscar Niemeyer, 1964

D'abord proposé au dix-huitième siècle dans un effort visant à mieux répartir les ressources nationales et à déconcentrer les investissements de Rio de Janeiro, le projet urbain de la ville de Brasilia a vu le jour dans les années 50 sous l'impulsion du Président Juscelino Kubitschek, à l'origine d'une véritable frénésie de travaux de construction. Des bâtiments innovants sont ainsi sortis de terre pour donner vie à une nouvelle capitale résolument tournée vers le progrès sous la direction des architectes Oscar Niemeyer et Lúcio Costa. Composé de deux tours de vingt-huit étages entourées de chaque côté par le Sénat en forme de coupole et par la Chambre des députés en forme de cuve, le Congresso Nacional forme le joyau architectural de ce site classé au patrimoine mondial de l'UNESCO.

Presentada inicialmente en el siglo XVIII como un esfuerzo por ampliar los recursos naturales y desplazar la concentración fuera de Río de Janeiro, la capital planificada de Brasilia fue realizada por el presidente Juscelino Kubitschek en la década de 1950. Inició un aluvión de construcciones y fue creando innovadores edificios, fiel reflejo de una nueva capital abierta y progresista, bajo la dirección de Óscar Niemeyer y Lúcio Costa. El *Congresso Nacional*, que consta de dos torres de 28 plantas flanqueadas por el Senado, en forma de cúpula, y la Cámara de los Diputados, en forma de cuenco, constituye la joya de la corona de este lugar, declarado Patrimonio de la Humanidad por la UNESCO.

Parliament Buildings, Stormont

Belfast, Northern Ireland
Arnold Thornely, 1932

At the end of the mile-long Prince of Wales Avenue, a dramatic statue of Unionist Home Rule campaigner Edward Carson beckons the visitor to Stormont. In 1921 this land was acquired for Northern Ireland's new parliament, following the Government of Ireland Act, granting the region self-government within the United Kingdom. Scaled back from a more ambitious plan following the Wall Street Crash, Thornely's classical edifice was built from Portland stone and mounted on Mourne granite. In 1972, the most devastating year of the Troubles, the parliament was abolished and direct rule from Westminster was reintroduced, but in 1998 the current Executive took its seat at Stormont as part of the Good Friday Agreement.

Am Ende der meilenlangen Prince of Wales Avenue reißt die energische Statue des Unionisten und Home-Rule-Aktivisten Edward Carson den Besucher förmlich nach Stormont. 1921 wurde dieses Land infolge des Government of Ireland Act für Nordirlands neues Parlament erworben, welcher der Region innerhalb des Vereinigten Königreichs Autonomie gewährte. Der klassische Bau Thornleys, dem aufgrund der Weltwirtschaftskrise ein weitaus ambitionierterer erster Entwurf Platz machen musste, wurde aus Portland-Stein und auf Mourne-Granit errichtet. 1972, dem schrecklichsten Jahr des Nordirlandkonflikts, wurde das Parlament abgeschafft und die Direktverwaltung durch Westminster erneuert, doch bezog 1998 die gegenwärtige Staatsführung Stormont im Zuge des Karfreitagsabkommens.

Au bout de la longue avenue Prince of Wales, une impressionnante statue du militant unioniste contre l'autonomie sous la tutelle de la couronne britannique, Edward Carson, invite le visiteur à pénétrer dans Stormont. Ce terrain fut acquis en 1921 pour le nouveau parlement d'Irlande du Nord, suite à la loi sur le Gouvernement de l'Irlande accordant à la région l'autonomie au sein du Royaume-Uni. Réduit par rapport au projet plus ambitieux au lendemain du krach boursier de 1929, l'édifice classique de Thornley a été construit en pierre de Portland et érigé sur du granit de Mourne. En 1972, année la plus dévastatrice du conflit nord-irlandais (les « Troubles »), le parlement fut aboli et le contrôle direct par Westminster réintroduit. Cependant, en 1998, le pouvoir alors en place établit son siège à Stormont suite à l'accord du Vendredi saint.

Al final de la avenida Prince of Wales, que se extiende a lo largo de kilómetro y medio, una espectacular estatua del defensor de la autonomía unionista, Edward Carson, atrae la mirada de los visitantes de Stormont En 1921, tras el Estatuto del Gobierno de Irlanda que otorgó a la región el autogobierno dentro del Reino Unido, se adquirió este terreno para la construcción del nuevo parlamento de Irlanda del Norte. Tras el Crac de Wall Street, que obligó a reducir su tamaño frente a un plan original más ambicioso, el edificio clásico de Thornley se construyó en piedra de Portland y granito de Mourne. En 1972, el año más devastador en la historia del conflicto de Irlanda del Norte, se abolió el parlamento y se reinstauró el gobierno directo por parte del Parlamento de Westminster pero, en 1998, el actual poder ejecutivo estableció su sede en Stormont tras el Acuerdo de Viernes Santo.

NO — ENTRY

Castile and León is the largest autonomous region in Spain, with a population of around 2.5 million and more World Heritage sites than any other area in the world. The offices of its government are located in the ancient heart of the city of Zamora. Its solid exterior wall, hewn from the same traditional stone as the Romanesque cathedral opposite, belies an airy, minimalist and innovative interior space, where two secret gardens flank a structure with an exclusively glass façade. The architect's dream was 'to build with air', and the realisation of his vision is a strikingly open and elegant government building.

Offices of the Castile and León Government

Zamora, Spain
Alberto Campo Baeza, 2012

Kastilien und León ist die größte autonome Gemeinschaft Spaniens; sie zählt rund 2,5 Millionen Einwohner und hat mehr Weltkulturerbestätten zu bieten als jede andere Gegend der Welt. Das Verwaltungsgebäude der Regionalregierung liegt in der historischen Altstadt Zamoras. Seine soliden Außenmauern, die aus demselben Stein gefügt wurden wie einst die gegenüberliegende romanische Kathedrale, umschließen einen luftigen, minimalistischen und innovativen Innenraum sowie zwei verborgene Gärten am Saum einer Anlage, die mit einer raffinierten Glasfassade aufwartet. Der Architekt hegte den Traum, „mit Luft zu bauen" und die Umsetzung seiner Vision ergab ein beeindruckend offenes und elegantes Regierungsgebäude.

Castille-et-León est la région autonome la plus grande d'Espagne, avec une population estimée à 2,5 millions d'habitants et plus de sites classés au patrimoine mondial qu'aucune autre région du globe. Son gouvernement siège dans l'ancien centre de la ville de Zamora. Ses solides remparts extérieurs, taillés dans la même pierre traditionnelle que celle de la cathédrale romane qui lui fait face, abritent un espace intérieur aéré, minimaliste et innovant où deux jardins secrets donnent sur une structure entièrement vitrée. L'architecte nourrissait l'ambition d'une « construction aérienne » incarnée par un bâtiment qui se distingue par une structure ouverte tout en élégance.

Castilla y León, la comunidad autónoma más grande de España, cuenta con una población de unos 2,5 millones de habitantes e incluye más lugares declarados Patrimonio de la Humanidad que cualquier otra parte del mundo. Su sede de gobierno se encuentra en el centro de la antigua ciudad de Zamora. Sus sólidos muros exteriores, construidos con la misma piedra tradicional que la catedral románica situada enfrente, ocultan un espacio interior amplio, minimalista e innovador, donde dos jardines secretos flanquean una estructura con una fachada totalmente acristalada. El sueño del arquitecto era «construir con aire» y su visión se ha materializado en un edificio gubernamental elegante y sorprendentemente abierto.

Following the growth of the Scottish National Party in the 1970s, and an eventual referendum in 1997 that saw the public vote in favour of bringing the majority of domestic affairs back under Scottish control, the vision of an independent Scottish Parliament was finally realised in 2004 with the unveiling of this striking building, which rises out from the rocks at the base of Arthur's Seat, linking the land and its people. This futuristic interpretation of Arts and Crafts architecture drew much criticism due to its indulgent budget, but it is now hailed as one of the most innovative spaces in the country.

Scottish Parliament Building

Edinburgh, Scotland
Enric Miralles, 2004

Im Zuge des Aufstiegs der Scottish National Party in den 1970er-Jahren sowie aufgrund des 1997 abgehaltenen Referendums, bei dem sich die Öffentlichkeit dafür aussprach, das Gros der innerstaatlichen Angelegenheiten wieder unter schottische Hoheit zurückzuführen, kam es im Jahr 2004 schließlich zur Umsetzung der Vision eines unabhängigen schottischen Parlaments. Das augenfällige Gebäude, welches sich aus dem Felsgestein am Fuß des Arthur's Seat erhebt, verbindet das Land und seine Menschen. Obwohl die nachsichtige Budgetdisziplin dieser futuristischen Interpretation von Arts-and-Crafts-Architektur eingangs einigen Unmut erregte, wird das Parlamentsgebäude heute doch als eine der innovativsten Stätten Schottlands gepriesen.

Suite au développement du parti national écossais dans les années 70, et à un référendum en 1997 dont le vote s'est soldé en faveur d'un contrôle écossais sur la majorité des affaires nationales, la vision d'un parlement écossais indépendant s'est finalement concrétisée en 2004 avec l'inauguration de ce bâtiment surprenant qui s'élève au-dessus des rochers au pied du Siège d'Arthur, liant le peuple à sa terre. Cette interprétation futuriste de l'art nouveau a suscité de nombreuses critiques en raison de son budget colossal. Elle est cependant désormais saluée comme l'un des espaces les plus innovants du pays.

Tras la expansión del Partido Nacional Escocés en la década de 1970 y el referéndum definitivo de 1997, que apoyó el retorno de la mayoría de los asuntos internos al control escocés, la visión de un parlamento de Escocia independiente se materializó finalmente en 2004, con la inauguración de este sorprendente edificio que surge de las rocas, al pie de la colina de Arthur's Seat, uniendo la tierra y sus habitantes. Esta interpretación futurista de la arquitectura Arts and Crafts suscitó numerosas críticas debido a un presupuesto muy permisivo pero, en la actualidad, es aclamado como uno de los espacios más innovadores del país.

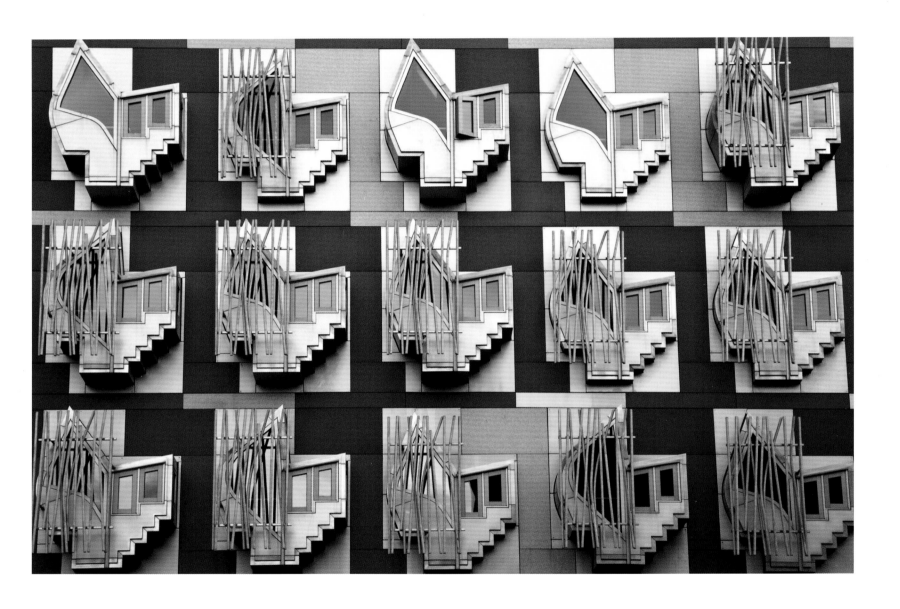

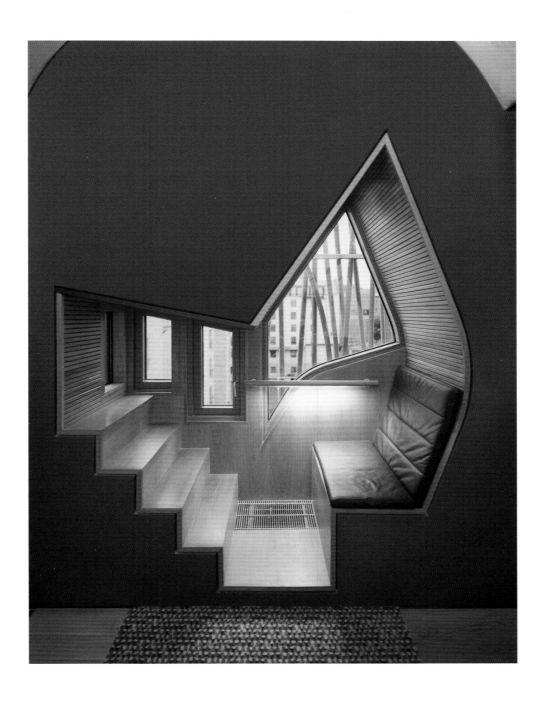

Senedd

Cardiff, Wales
Rogers Stirk Harbour + Partners, 2006

Cardiff Bay was once the nucleus of Wales's vital coal-exporting industry. Now it is home to the Welsh National Assembly, which was formed as a result of the 1997 referendum, and its architecture, with its abundance of glass, Welsh slate, and natural ventilation, is a bold testament to the potential of regeneration. The Senedd is dominated by a beautifully sculpted roof, both externally and internally, where it descends dramatically upon the chamber, and according to the Assembly, the building's principles of accessibility, transparency and sustainability perfectly mirror those for which the Assembly itself strives for the Welsh people.

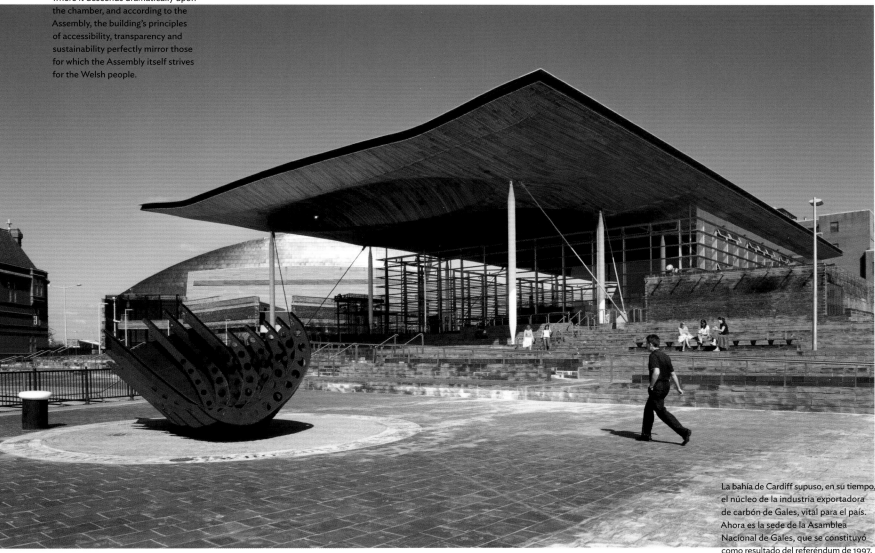

La bahía de Cardiff supuso, en su tiempo, el núcleo de la industria exportadora de carbón de Gales, vital para el país. Ahora es la sede de la Asamblea Nacional de Gales, que se constituyó como resultado del referéndum de 1997. Su arquitectura, con gran abundancia de cristal, pizarra galesa y ventilación natural, representa un testimonio audaz del potencial de regeneración. El Senedd está dominado por un tejado bellamente esculpido, tanto en el interior como en el exterior, que desciende de manera espectacular hasta la cámara. Según la Asamblea, los principios del edificio de accesibilidad, transparencia y sostenibilidad reflejan a la perfección los mismos principios que defiende la Asamblea para el pueblo galés.

Die Bucht von Cardiff bildete einst das Herzstück der lebenswichtigen walisischen Kohlenexporte. Heute befindet sich dort die Nationalversammlung für Wales, die aus dem 1997 abgehaltenen Referendum hervorging. Ihre an Glas und walisischem Schiefer so reiche und natürlich belüftete Bauweise bekennt sich deutlich zum Potenzial der Erneuerung. Der Senedd wird Innen wie Außen von seinem wunderschön gestalteten Dach beherrscht, das sich beeindruckend zum Plenarsaal hin wölbt. Laut Nationalversammlung spiegle die Zugänglichkeit, Transparenz und Nachhaltigkeit des Senedd jene Prinzipien wider, deren Umsetzung sich das walisische Parlament zum Wohle des eigenen Volkes verschrieben habe.

La Baie de Cardiff était autrefois le centre névralgique des exportations de charbon gallois. Elle abrite aujourd'hui l'Assemblée nationale du pays de Galles, établie à l'issue du référendum de 1997. Son architecture, marquée par l'abondance de verre et d'ardoise galloise, et sa ventilation naturelle incarnent la vision audacieuse d'un renouveau aux multiples possibilités. La Senedd est dominée par un magnifique toit sculpté, à l'intérieur comme à l'extérieur, offrant un cadre spectaculaire au-dessus de la salle et, de là à à l'Assemblée. Les principes ayant sous-tendu la construction de l'édifice, à savoir l'accessibilité, la transparence et le développement durable, sont en parfaite adéquation avec les valeurs que l'Assemblée défend dans l'intérêt du peuple gallois.

The Palace of Westminster, home to the House of Commons and the House of Lords, stands on the site of a medieval predecessor that was destroyed by fire in 1834. Two years later, Barry won the commission to build a new palace, and working closely with Pugin, he paid particular attention to the extant features and blended them into the new edifice. Construction on the Perpendicular Gothic complex began in 1840, only to be completed thirty years later. The Palace of Westminster – particularly the Big Ben clock tower, which has been functioning since 1859 – has become a globally acknowledged symbol of England, and in 1987 it was declared a UNESCO World Heritage Site.

Der Palace of Westminster, der das House of Commons und das House of Lords beherbergt, erhebt sich am früheren Standort einer mittelalterlichen Anlage, die bei einem Brand im Jahr 1834 zerstört wurde. Zwei Jahr später wurde Barry mit der Errichtung eines neuen Palastes beauftragt, den er in enger Zusammenarbeit mit Pugin und unter strengster Berücksichtigung und harmonischer Eingliederung der noch vorhandenen Elemente in den neuen Entwurf errichtete. Die Bauarbeiten an diesem im spätgotischen *Perpendicular*-Stil gehaltenen Gebäudekomplex begannen 1840 und endeten bereits drei Jahre später. Der Palace of Westminster – insbesondere der Glockenturm des Big Ben, der 1859 das erste Mal erklang – wurde zu einem weltweit anerkannten Wahrzeichen Englands und 1987 schließlich ins UNESCO-Weltkulturerbe aufgenommen.

Palace of Westminster

London, England
Charles Barry & Augustus Pugin, 1870

Le Palais de Westminster, siège de la Chambre des communes et de la Chambre des Lords, se dresse sur l'ancien site d'un édifice médiéval détruit par un incendie en 1834. Deux ans plus tard, Barry remporte le concours pour ériger un nouveau palais. En étroite collaboration avec Pugin, Barry a plus particulièrement veillé à préserver les éléments existants pour les intégrer au nouvel édifice. Les travaux du complexe perpendiculaire de style gothique ont débuté en 1840 pour ne s'achever que trente ans plus tard. Le Palais de Westminster, et notamment la tour de l'horloge Big Ben, qui fonctionne depuis 1859, est devenu un symbole mondialement connu de l'Angleterre, et a été inscrit au patrimoine mondial de l'Unesco en 1987.

El Palacio de Westminster, sede de la Cámara de los Comunes y de la Cámara de los Lores, se encuentra en el emplazamiento de un antiguo edificio medieval, destruido por un incendio en 1834. Dos años más tarde, Barry recibió el encargo de crear un nuevo palacio y, en estrecha colaboración con Pugin, dedicó una atención especial a las características existentes y las incluyó en el nuevo edificio. La construcción del conjunto gótico perpendicular, que comenzó en 1840, finalizó solo treinta años más tarde. El Palacio de Westminster, y en particular la torre del reloj del Big Ben, que ha estado en funcionamiento desde 1859, se ha convertido en un símbolo de Inglaterra reconocido mundialmente y en 1987 fue declarado Patrimonio de la Humanidad por la UNESCO.

City Hall

London, England
Foster + Partners, 2002

Die Errichtung der neuen Londoner City Hall begann im Jahr 1998 als Teil des Entwicklungsprojekts „More London", das sich der Nutzbarmachung der Flächen zwischen der London Bridge und der Tower Bridge verschrieben hatte. Das knollenförmige Gebäude setzt Ideen um, die bereits in Fosters Reichstagsentwurf aufgekeimt waren; seine vollkommen aus Glas bestehende Fassade erzeugt Transparenz und fördert den Austausch mit der umliegenden Stadt. Im Gebäudeinneren schraubt sich ein 500 Meter langer Wendelgang durch alle zehn Stockwerke bis nach oben und besonderes Augenmerk wurde auf Umweltfaktoren gelegt: So wurde die neue City Hall in einem Winkel errichtet, der zu starke direkte Sonneneinstrahlung vermeiden hilft und tragen außerdem Photovoltaikpanele zur Verringerung des Stromverbrauchs bei, wodurch das neue Londoner Rathaus zu den umweltfreundlichsten Gebäuden der Stadt gehört.

Construction of the new City Hall in London began in 1998, as part of the More London development project, which was introduced to utilise the space between London Bridge and Tower Bridge. Bulbous in shape, the building develops ideas that germinated in Foster's Reichstag design; its entirely glass façade engenders transparency and promotes interaction with the surrounding city. Internally, a helical walkway ascends all ten storeys, measuring 500 metres in total, and particular attention was paid to environmental factors: it is built at an angle to avoid intense direct sunlight, and solar panels also serve to reduce electricity consumption, making it one of London's greenest buildings.

Les travaux de construction du nouveau City Hall (Hôtel de ville) de Londres débutèrent en 1998, dans le cadre du projet de développement baptisé More London, dont l'objectif était d'exploiter les espaces situés entre London Bridge et Tower Bridge. En forme de bulbe, l'édifice incarne des idées tout droit inspirées du Reichstag de Foster ; sa façade entièrement vitrée apporte de la transparence tout en encourageant les échanges avec la ville avoisinante. À l'intérieur, une passerelle en colimaçon dessert les dix étages de l'édifice qui mesure en tout 500 mètres. L'écologie y est particulièrement mise à l'honneur : le bâtiment est incliné de manière à éviter une exposition directe et intense à la lumière du soleil, et des panneaux solaires permettent également de réduire la facture électrique, ce qui en fait l'un des bâtiments les plus écologiques de Londres.

La construcción del nuevo Ayuntamiento de Londres, el City Hall, comenzó en 1998, como parte del proyecto de desarrollo «More London», que se creó para aprovechar el espacio entre London Bridge y Tower Bridge. El edificio, en forma de bulbo, materializa unas ideas que germinaron en el diseño del Reichstag de Foster. Su fachada totalmente acristalada irradia transparencia y favorece la interacción con la ciudad circundante. En el interior, una pasarela helicoidal de 500 metros asciende por las diez plantas. Se ha prestado una atención especial a los factores medioambientales: se construyó inclinado para evitar la intensa luz solar directa y los paneles solares ayudan a reducir el consumo eléctrico, lo que acredita este edificio como uno de los más ecológicos de Londres.

The Palais Bourbon, the seat of the National Assembly, was built for the Duchesse de Bourbon, daughter of Louis XIV. Initially it was composed of a principal block with simple wings, inspired by the Grand Trianon de Versailles, but it has been extensively renovated in its lifetime. In 1756, it was purchased by the Prince de Condé, who developed the site between 1764 and 1789, and in 1808 the familiar portico by Bernard Poyet was added to the façade. Inside, the palace's library is a particular highlight: completed in 1847, the ceiling was painted by Delacroix, and it houses priceless references, including the minutes of the trial of Joan of Arc.

Das Palais Bourbon, der Sitz der französischen Nationalversammlung, wurde für die Herzogin de Bourbon, einer Tochter Ludwig XIV., errichtet. Anfangs bestand der durch das Grand Trianon in Versailles inspirierte Bau aus einem zentralen Gebäudekomplex einschließlich schlichter Flügel, doch wurde es zeit seines Bestehens immer wieder ausgiebig renoviert. Im Jahr 1756 erwarb der Prince de Condé das Palais und gestaltete es zwischen 1764 und 1789 nach seinen Vorstellungen um; 1808 wurde die Fassade schließlich um den bekannten Portikus von Bernard Poyet erweitert. Im Gebäudeinneren stellt vor allem die Palastbibliothek ein ganz besonderes Kleinod dar: Die Decke des 1847 fertiggestellten Raums wurde von Delacroix gemalt und hier befinden sich unschätzbare Zeugnisse, darunter die Protokolle der Verurteilung Jeanne d'Arcs.

Palais Bourbon

Paris, France
Lorenzo Giardini, 1728

Le Palais Bourbon, siège de l'Assemblée nationale, a été construit pour la Duchesse de Bourbon, fille de Louis XIV. À l'origine composé d'un bâtiment principal doté d'ailes simples, le Palais Bourbon a été inspiré par le Grand Trianon de Versailles. Au fil du temps, il a toutefois été remanié en profondeur. Le Palais fut racheté en 1756 par le Prince de Condé, qui développa le site entre 1764 et 1789. En 1808, le fameux portique de Bernard Poyet fut ajouté à la façade. À l'intérieur, la bibliothèque du palais offre certainement le clou de la visite : achevé en 1847, le plafond est l'œuvre du peintre Delacroix. La bibliothèque possède en outre des ouvrages inestimables, dont les comptes-rendus d'audiences du procès de Jeanne d'Arc.

El Palais Bourbon, sede de la Asamblea Nacional, se construyó por orden de la duquesa de Bourbon, hija de Luis XIV. En principio, estaba formado por un bloque principal de alas sencillas, inspirado en el Gran Trianón de Versalles, pero ha sido renovado en profundidad a lo largo de toda su vida. En 1756, fue adquirido por el príncipe de Condé, que amplió el sitio entre 1764 y 1789. En 1808 se añadió a la fachada el conocido pórtico de Bernard Poyet. En su interior, destaca en particular la biblioteca del palacio: el techo, finalizado en 1847, es obra de Delacroix y la sala alberga valiosísimas referencias, incluidas las actas del juicio de Juana de Arco.

Palais Bourbon, Paris, France

Het Binnenhof

The Hague, The Netherlands
Early 13th century

The coastal city of The Hague is the current seat of government of the Netherlands. It is famous for dealing with international affairs and this can be traced back to the seventeenth century, when the Dutch Republic played a central role in Europe and thus became a centre for diplomatic negotiations. Indeed, The Hague boasts one of the most stable political parliaments in the world. The Binnenhof hosts the meetings between both houses of the state and the office of the Prime Minister. Construction on the Gothic castle complex began in the thirteenth century, and it is now known as one of the oldest houses of parliament in the world.

Die Seestadt Den Haag beherbergt den Regierungssitz der Niederlande. Sie ist berühmt für ihre langjährige Erfahrung im Umgang mit internationalen Angelegenheiten, die sich bis ins 17. Jahrhundert zurückverfolgen lässt, als die Republik der Niederlande eine zentrale Stellung innerhalb Europas einnahm und Den Haag zum Zentrum diplomatischer Verhandlungen aufstieg. Noch heute darf sich die niederländische Hauptstadt zurecht eines der altehrwürdigsten Regierungssitze der Welt rühmen. Der Binnenhof dient den beiden Kammern des Staates sowie dem Büro des Ministerpräsidenten als Verhandlungsort. Die Grundsteinlegung zum gothischen Schlosskomplex erfolgte bereits im 13. Jahrhundert und der *Innenhof* gilt als eines der ältesten Parlamentsgebäude der Welt.

Het Binnenhof, The Hague, The Netherlands

La ville côtière de la Haye abrite le siège actuel du gouvernement des Pays-Bas. La ville est également connue pour son rôle dans les litiges internationaux, une tradition qui remonte au dix-septième siècle, lorsque la République néerlandaise occupait une place prépondérante en Europe qui lui valut de devenir un centre pour les négociations diplomatiques. La Haye peut de ce fait se targuer d'héberger l'un des parlements politiques les plus stables du monde. Le Binnenhof héberge les réunions entre les deux chambres des États généraux et des bureaux du Premier ministre. La construction de l'enceinte du château gothique a débuté au treizième siècle. Le Binnenhof est aujourd'hui connu pour abriter l'une des chambres parlementaires les plus anciennes au monde.

En la ciudad costera de La Haya se encuentra la sede actual del Gobierno de los Países Bajos. Es famosa por tratar asuntos internacionales, hecho que se puede remontar hasta el siglo XVII, cuando la República de Holanda desempeñó un papel crucial en Europa y se convirtió en un centro de negociaciones diplomáticas. En efecto, La Haya se enorgullece de tener uno de los parlamentos políticos más estables del mundo. En el Binnenhof se celebran las reuniones entre las dos cámaras de representantes y se encuentra el despacho del primer ministro. El conjunto del castillo gótico, cuya construcción se inició en el siglo XIII, es conocido actualmente como una de las cámaras parlamentarias más antiguas del mundo.

The Louise Weiss Building is the principal structure in a complex constructed to accommodate the growing Parliament of the European Union. This building houses assembly rooms, more than one thousand parliamentary offices, and an impressive modern hemicycle, where members meet monthly for plenary sessions, encircled by bands of interpreter booths separated from the public gallery above by a wall of lights. The architects were inspired by the history and future of Europe; the design owes a debt to Roman amphitheatres, and the evolution of democracy is signified by the deliberately 'unfinished' ellipse at the top of the 60-metre tower. Eurosceptics, however, have aligned it more to Bruegel's 'Tower of Babel'.

Beim Louise-Weiss-Gebäude handelt es sich um den zentralen Bau jener Anlage, die zur Unterbringung des wachsenden Europäischen Parlaments errichtet wurde. In diesem Bau sind neben Sitzungssälen über tausend Parlamentsbüros und ein beeindruckender moderner Plenarsaal untergebracht, der Abgeordneten für ihre allmonatlichen Plenarsitzungen dient. Umrahmt wird dieser von Reihen an Dolmetschkabinen, die durch eine Lichterwand von der Zuschauertribüne getrennt sind. Die Architekten inspirierten sich an der Vergangenheit und an der Zukunft Europas: Der Entwurf erinnert an römische Amphitheater und die Entstehung der Demokratie, symbolisiert durch die bewusst „unfertige" Ellipse des 60 Meter hohen Turms – wenngleich Euroskeptiker darin viel mehr Bruegels *Turmbau zu Babel* zu erkennen glauben.

Le bâtiment Louise Weiss forme la structure principale d'un complexe destiné à accueillir le Parlement grandissant de l'Union européenne. Cet édifice abrite des salles de réunion, plus d'un millier de bureaux parlementaires, et un impressionnant hémicycle moderne, où les députés se réunissent tous les mois en séances plénières, encerclé dans sa partie supérieure par les cabines d'interprètes dissimulées de la tribune par un mur de lumière. L'histoire de l'Europe et son avenir ont largement inspiré les architectes dont les travaux doivent beaucoup aux amphithéâtres romains. L'évolution de la démocratie y est suggérée par l'ellipse délibérément « inachevée » en haut de la tour de 60 mètres. Les eurosceptiques n'ont cependant pas tardé à rapprocher l'ouvrage de la *Tour de Babel* de Bruegel.

El edificio Louise Weiss constituye la principal estructura de un complejo construido para albergar el Parlamento, en creciente expansión, de la Unión Europea. Este edificio comprende salones de actos, más de un millar de oficinas parlamentarias y un impresionante hemiciclo moderno, donde los miembros se reúnen una vez al mes para las sesiones plenarias, rodeado por las cabinas de los intérpretes y separado de la galería pública superior por una pared luminosa. Los arquitectos se inspiraron en la historia y el futuro de Europa: el diseño tiene una gran deuda con los anfiteatros romanos. La evolución de la democracia está representada por la elipse deliberadamente «inacabada» de la cima de la torre que mide 60 metros. Los euroescépticos, no obstante, lo equiparan más con la *Torre de Babel* de Bruegel.

Louise Weiss Building

Strasbourg, France
Architecture-Studio, 1999

Louise Weiss Building, Strasbourg, France

Palazzo Lombardia

Milan, Italy
Pei Cobb Freed & Partners, 2010

Lombardy is the wealthiest and most populous region in Italy, and this award-winning development is the product of the decision to construct efficient, accessible administrative government offices that would employ cutting-edge green practices and create attractive outdoor space. The result is striking but subtle in its complexity. Its distinctive form is composed of interlacing threads of office space from which the slender 131-metre tower emerges. The building utilises a broad array of green features, including an active climate wall, which tempers light and heat, and its flowing forms enfold the Piazza Città di Lombardia, a public space covered with a transparent, lightweight canopy.

Die Lombardei ist die wohlhabendste und bevölkerungsreichste Region Italiens. Diese preisgekrönte Entwicklung verdankt sich der Entscheidung zur Errichtung effizienter und zugänglicher Verwaltungs- bzw. Regierungsgebäude, der Umsetzung wegbereitender grüner Praktiken und der Anlage ansprechender Außenflächen. Das Ergebnis ist markant und in seiner Komplexität geradezu subtil. Die unverwechselbare Form des Palazzo Lombardia besteht aus ineinander verflochtenen Bändern aus Büroflächen, aus denen ein schlanker und 131 Meter hoher Turm aufragt. Das Gebäude verfügt über eine Reihe grüner Merkmale, darunter eine aktive Klimawand zur Licht- und Hitzeminderung, und seine fließenden Formen umschlingen den mit einer durchsichtigen und schier schwerelosen Überdachung bekrönten öffentlichen Raum der Piazza Città di Lombardia.

La Lombardie est la région la plus riche et la plus connue d'Italie. L'aménagement de cet édifice exemplaire est le fruit d'un parti pris : celui de construire un ensemble de bureaux publics et administratifs efficace et accessible, à la pointe des pratiques écologiques, tout en aménageant d'agréables espaces extérieurs. Le résultat est d'autant plus remarquable que la complexité de l'édifice parvient à se faire oublier. Sa structure reconnaissable entre toutes se compose d'un réseau entrelacé d'espaces administratifs dont émerge la tour longiligne de 131 mètres. L'édifice arbore un grand nombre de fonctionnalités écologiques, dont un mur climatique actif qui atténue la lumière et la chaleur. Ses courbes fluides bordent la Piazza Citât di Lombardi, un espace public couvert par un auvent à la transparence aérienne.

La Lombardía, la región más rica y poblada de Italia, se enorgullece de su desarrollo triunfal, resultado de la decisión de construir unas oficinas de administración pública eficientes y accesibles, que aplican unas prácticas ecológicas de vanguardia y crean un atractivo espacio exterior. El conjunto resulta de una complejidad llamativa y sutil. Su forma característica está compuesta por filas interrelacionadas de oficinas entre las cuales sobresale la esbelta torre de 131 metros. El edificio saca partido de una amplia gama de funciones ecológicas, incluida una pared climática activa, que atenúa la luz y el calor. Sus formas fluidas envuelven la Piazza Città di Lombardia, un espacio público con una cubierta ligera y transparente.

Parliament of the Principality of Liechtenstein

Vaduz, Liechtenstein
Studio Hansjörg Göritz, 2008

Liechtenstein, with an area of just over 160 square kilometres and a population of 35,000, is arguably the richest country in the world. Its parliament, however, has a timeless, spare aesthetic, with just the slightest undertones of theatricality. Set in a stunning location on Peter Kaiser Square, under a looming, verdant Alpine slope, a million custom-made bricks were used in its construction. The centrepieces of the complex are the Landtag's assembly hall, with its 18-metre-high pitched roof, and the roof terrace, which offers a breath-taking panorama of the Swiss mountains.

Mit einem Staatsgebiet von nur rund 160 Quadratkilometern und einer Bevölkerung um die 35.000 ist Liechtenstein wohl das reichste Land der Erde. Sein Parlament dagegen weist eine zeitlose, schlichte Ästhetik auf, bereichert lediglich um die zartesten theatralischen Unertöne. Bei der Errichtung des atemberaubend am Peter-Kaiser-Platz und unter einem aufragenden Alpenhang gelegenen Landtages kamen eine Million maßgefertigte Ziegel zum Einsatz. Die beiden Herzstücke der Anlage bilden der Plenarsaal des Landtags mit seinem 18 Meter hohen Spitzdach sowie die Dachterrasse, die beeindruckende Aussichten auf die Schweizer Bergwelt erlaubt.

Le Liechtenstein, avec une superficie d'à peine plus de 160 kilomètres carrés pour 35 000 habitants, est sans conteste le pays le plus riche du monde. Une opulence toutefois absente de son parlement au style aussi intemporel que sobre, un brin théâtral. Avec pour écrin la magnifique place Peter Kaiser, en contrebas d'un versant alpin verdoyant, le parlement arbore un million de briques faites sur mesure. Le complexe s'articule autour de deux pièces maîtresses : la salle de l'Assemblée du Langtag avec sa toiture en pente de 18 mètres de haut, et la terrasse sur toit avec sa vue panoramique des Alpes suisses à couper le souffle.

Parliament of the Principality of Liechtenstein, Vaduz, Liechtenstein

Liechtenstein, con una superficie ligeramente superior a 160 kilómetros cuadrados y una población de 35.000 habitantes, es posiblemente el país más rico del mundo. Su parlamento, no obstante, presenta una estética intemporal y sobria, con solo unos sutiles toques de teatralidad. Esta construcción, situada en un enclave deslumbrante de la plaza de Peter Kaiser, al pie de una pendiente alpina verde e imponente, requirió un millón de ladrillos hechos a medida. Las partes más destacadas del complejo arquitectónico son la sala de la asamblea del Landtag, con un tejado a dos aguas de 18 metros de altura, y la terraza de la azotea, que proporciona unas vistas panorámicas impresionantes de las montañas suizas.

Reichstag Building

Berlin, Germany
Paul Wallot, 1894
Norman Foster, 1999

Dem Deutschen Volke – 'To the German People'. This famous inscription, added to the Reichstag's façade in 1916, has survived many tumultuous times. Devastated by a 1933 arson attack, Wallot's original High Renaissance building stood idle for a long period after the Second World War, during which it suffered extensive damage. Partial renovation was carried out mid-century, but it wasn't until the 1990s, with the reunification of Germany, that the Reichstag was reinstated as the seat of government. Foster's subsequent reconstruction included the insertion of a new dome that provides light and ventilation to the debating chamber, but, more significantly, allows the public to watch democracy in progress below.

Dem Deutschen Volke. Diese berühmte Inschrift, die der Fassade des Reichstags im Jahr 1916 hinzugefügt wurde, hat wahrlich turbulente Zeiten überdauert. Das von Wallot im Stil der Neorenaissance errichtete Gebäude wurde 1933 durch Brandstiftung zerstört, im Zuge des zweiten Weltkriegs beinahe vollständig verheert und blieb nach dessen Ende lange Zeit ungenutzt. Zwar erfolgte in der Mitte des letzten Jahrhunderts eine teilweise Renovierung, doch dauerte es bis zur deutschen Wiedervereinigung in den 1990er-Jahren, dass die deutsche Regierung erneut an diesen Ort zurückkehrte. Der nachfolgende Umbau durch Foster fügte dem Ganzen eine neue, dem Plenarsaal Licht spendene und Luftigkeit verleihende Kuppel hinzu, deren zweifelsfrei wichtigste Funktion es ist, Besuchern einen Blick auf das Entstehen von Demokratie zu ermöglichen.

Dem Deutschen Volke – « Au peuple allemand ». Cette célèbre devise inscrite sur la façade du Reichstag en 1916 a traversé bien des tumultes. Dévasté par un incendie d'origine criminelle en 1933, l'édifice original conçu par Wallot dans un style néoclassique est longtemps resté sans emploi après la Seconde Guerre mondiale, pendant laquelle il a subi d'importants dégâts. Une rénovation partielle fut entreprise vers le milieu du siècle, mais ce ne fut que dans les années 90, avec la réunification de l'Allemagne, que le Reichstag fut rétabli dans sa fonction de siège du gouvernement. Les travaux de reconstruction entrepris par la suite par Foster ont permis d'aménager un nouveau dôme venant éclairer et ventiler l'hémicycle, et mieux encore, invitant le public à contempler la démocratie à l'œuvre.

Dem Deutschen Volke – «Al pueblo alemán». Esta famosa inscripción, colocada en la fachada del Reichstag en 1916, ha sobrevivido a épocas tumultuosas. Destruido en 1933 por un incendio provocado, el edificio del alto renacimiento original de Wallot estuvo en desuso durante largo tiempo después de la Segunda Guerra Mundial, período en el que sufrió innumerables daños. A mediados del siglo se llevó a cabo una renovación parcial del Reichstag, pero no se rehabilitó como sede de gobierno hasta la década de 1990, con la reunificación de Alemania. La posterior reconstrucción de Foster incluía la colocación de una nueva cúpula que proporcionara luz y ventilación a la cámara de debates y, lo que es aún mas importante, permitiera al público observar más abajo la democracia en progreso.

Photography Credits

Austrian Parliament Building
p. 12/3 © Martin Ruegner/
Getty Images
p. 14 © Yadid Levy/Getty Images
p. 15 © Scott E. Barbour/
Getty Images
p. 16/7 © Jorge Royan/Alamy

Parliament House, Stockholm
p. 18/9 © mos-photography/
Getty Images
p. 20 © bednarek-art.com/Alamy
p. 21 © Elvele Images Ltd/Alamy
p. 22/3 © Werner Nystrand/
Getty Images

South African Houses of Parliament
p. 24 © Jeremy Woodhouse/
Getty Images
p. 25 © W. Robert Moore/
National Geographic
Creative
p. 26 © imageBROKER/Alamy
p. 27 © imageBROKER/Alamy

Hungarian Parliament Building
p. 28/9 © Hlinkazsolt/
Getty Images
p. 30 © Goran Bogicevic/
Shutterstock
p. 31 © T photography/
Shutterstock

Old Royal Palace, Athens
p. 32 © Marco Simoni/
Getty Images
p. 33 © Konstantinos Tsakalidis/
Alamy
p. 34/5 © Alvis Upitis,
Photographer's Choice RF/
Getty Images

Palace of Parliament, Bucharest
p. 36/7 © Atlantide Phototravel/
Corbis
p. 38 © Narcis/age fotostock
p. 39 © Walter Bibikow/
age fotostock
p. 40/1 Danita Delimont/
Getty Images

Union Buildings, Pretoria
p. 42/3 © Hoberman/age fotostock
p. 44 © Florian Kopp/
imageBROKER/
age fotostock
p. 45 © J. Countess/
Contributor/Getty Images

The Knesset Building
p. 46 © Spaces Images/Alamy
p. 47 © Moment Editorial/
Getty Images
p. 48 © Jeremy Woodhouse,
Blend Images/Getty Images
p. 49 © Dmitry Pistrov/
Shutterstock

Moscow Kremlin
p. 50/1 © Michael Runkel Robert
Harding World Imagery/
Getty Images
p. 52 © De Agostini/
W. BussDe Agostini
Picture Library/Getty Images
p. 53 © RIA Novosti/Alamy
p. 54/5 © ID1974 / Shutterstock

African Union Conference Center
p. 56 © AFP/Stringer/
Getty Images
p. 57 © Dereje Belachew/Alamy
p. 58 © ArtPix/Alamy
p. 59 © Dereje Belachew/Alamy

Georgian Parliament Building
p. 60 © PSI/Alamy
p. 61 © Tomasz Bidermann/
Shutterstock
p. 62/3 © Vano Shlamov/Stringer/
Getty Images

Government House of Baku
p. 64/5 © Budi, G Wimmer/
age fotostock
p. 66 © Alexey Zarubin/Alamy
p. 67 © Magdalena
Paluchowska/Alamy

Mazhilis Parliament Building
p. 68/9 © Jane Sweeney
Photographer's Choice RF/
Getty Images
p. 70 © Jane Sweeney
The Image Bank/
Getty Images
p. 71 © Elena Mirage/
Shutterstock

Sansad Bhavan
p. 72/3 © Travel Ink Gallo Images/
Getty Images
p. 74 © Bildgentur-Online/
age fotostock
p. 75 © Prakash Singh/Staff/
Getty Images

Jatiyo Sangshad Bhaban
p. 76/7 © Mahmud Fahmi/
Getty Images
p. 78 © Eye Ubiquitous/
Contributor / Getty Images
p. 79 © Robin Laurance/Alamy

Ho Chi Minh City Hall
p. 80/1 © Gerhard Zwerger-
Schoner/imageBROKER/
age fotostock

**New Sarawak State Legislative Assembly
(DUN) Building**
p. 82/3 © Andrew Watson
Photolibrary/Getty Images
p. 84/5 © Andrew Watson/
Getty Image

Great Hall of the People
p. 86/7 © KokoroImages.com
Moment/Getty Images
p. 88/9 © Digital Vision.
Photodisc/Getty Images
p. 90 © Frederic J. Brown/staff/
Getty Images
p. 91 © Luis Castaneda Inc.
The Image Bank/
Getty Images

Mansudae Assembly Hall
p. 92/3 © KCNA KCNA/Reuters

National Assembly Building, Seoul
p. 94/5 © TongRo Images/
Getty Images
p. 96/7 © Noon Tabtimdaeng
Moment Open/
Getty Images

**Tokyo Metropolitan Government
Building**
p. 98 © Sean Pavone/Alamy
p. 99 © Takamex/Shutterstock
p. 100 © Tomas Riehle/
ARTUR IMAGES
p. 101 © Takamex/Shutterstock

Parliament House, Canberra
p. 102/3 © David Messent/
Getty Images
p. 104 © David Coleman/Alamy
p. 105 © Arcaid Images/Alamy

Parliament Buildings, Wellington
p. 106/7 © travellinglight/Alamy

Los Angeles City Hall
p. 108/9 © Peter Schickert/
age fotostock
p. 110 © SiliconValleyStock/Alamy
p. 111 © Jon Arnold Images Ltd/
Alamy

National Palace, Mexico
p. 112/3 © Borna_Mirahmadian/
Shutterstock
p. 114 © RosaIreneBetancourt 7/
Alamy
p. 115 © David R. Frazier
Photolibrary, Inc./Alamy

National Capitol Building, Cuba
p. 116/7 © Grant Rooney/
age fotostock
p. 118 © VPC Photo/Alamy
p. 119 © Nick Brooks/Alamy

Toronto City Hall
p. 120/1 © Naibank/Getty Images
p. 122 © Design Pics Inc/Alamy
p. 123 © Wolfgang Kaehler/
Contributor/Getty Images

United States Capitol
p. 124/5 © Steve Heap/Shutterstock
p. 126 © Brian Jannsen/Alamy
p. 127 © All Canada Photos/Alamy

Parliament Buildings, Ottawa
p. 128/9 © Miles Ertman/
Getty Images
p. 130 © Marshall Ikonography/
Alamy
p. 131 © Jiawangkun/Shutterstock
p. 132/3 © Naibank/Getty Images

La Casa Rosada
p. 134 © Jason Edwards
National Geographic/
Getty Images
p. 135 © Ralf Hettler/
Getty Images

National Congress Building, Brasília
p. 136/7 © Bruce Yuanyue Bi/
Getty Images
p. 138 © Barbara Staubach/
ARTUR IMAGES
p. 139 © Barbara Staubach/
ARTUR IMAGES

Parliament Buildings, Stormont
p. 140/1 © Surfin Chef –
scImages.me.uk/
Getty Images
p. 142 © scenicireland.com/
Christopher Hill
Photographic/Alamy
p. 143 © Design Pics/
Peter Zoeller Design Pics/
Getty Images

**Offices of the Castile and León
Government**
p. 144 © Javier Callejas
p. 145 © Javier Callejas
p. 146/7 © Javier Callejas

Scottish Parliament Building
p. 148/9 © Roy Henderson/
Shutterstock
p. 150 © Kathy Collins
Photographer's Choice/
Getty Images
p. 151 © Roland Halbe/
ARTUR IMAGES
p. 152 © John McKenna/Alamy
p. 153 © Roland Halbe/
ARTUR IMAGES

Senedd
p. 154 © Edmund Sumner/
ARTUR IMAGES
p. 155 © ffoto_travel/Alamy

Palace of Westminster
p. 156/7 © John and Tina Reid
Moment/Getty Images
p. 158 © Arcaid Images/Alamy
p. 159 © Arcaid Images/Alamy

City Hall, London
p. 160 © Pisaphotography/
Shutterstock
p. 161 © DBURKE/Alamy
p. 162 © John Wheeler/Alamy
p. 163 © Vulture Labs Moment/
Getty Images

Palais Bourbon
p. 164/5 © DUCEPT Pascal/
hemis.fr hemis.fr/
Getty Images
p. 166 © LMR Group/Alamy
p. 167 © LOOK Die Bildagentur
der Fotografen GmbH/
Alamy

Het Binnenhof
p. 168 © Sash Alexander
Photography Moment/
Getty Images
p. 169 © Bildarchiv Monheim
GmbH/Alamy
p. 170/1 © Tim Draper Dorling
Kindersley/Getty Images

Louise Weiss Building
p. 172 © Shaun Egan AWL Images/
Getty Images
p. 173 © Murat Taner
Photographer's Choice/
Getty Images
p. 174/5 © Marco Vacca
Photographer's Choice RF/
Getty Images

Palazzo Lombardia
p. 176 © Stuart Paton Photodisc/
Getty Images
p. 177 © Valentino Visentini/
Alamy
p. 178/9 © Simone Becchetti/
Getty Images

**Parliament of the Principality of
Liechtenstein**
p. 180 © Jürg Zürcher
p. 181 © Jürg Zürcher
p. 182 © Jürg Zürcher
p. 183 © Jürg Zürcher

Reichstag Building
p. 184 © fhm Moment/
Getty Images
p. 185 © Werner Huthmacher/
ARTUR IMAGES
p. 186 © Lexan/Shutterstock
p. 187 © Zap Art/
The Image Bank/
Getty Images

Libraries
9781909399105

Theatres
9781909399112

Gardens
9781909399440

Government
9781909399457